AMERICAN WAR NARRATIVES
1917-1918

AMERICAN
WAR
NARRATIVES
1917-1918

A STUDY

AND BIBLIOGRAPHY

CHARLES V. GENTHE

DAVID LEWIS   NEW YORK

ACKNOWLEDGMENTS

The library staffs at Washington State University, California State College at Long Beach, Chico State College, the University of California at Los Angeles and the California State Library were most helpful in assisting me in obtaining many scarce books. Professors Lewis Buchanan, Charles Blackburn and Raymond Muse of Washington State University willingly gave of their time to assist me on this project when it was still a doctoral dissertation. Special thanks go to Joan Ostlund, Barnard Flynn and Leonard Kent for their assistance in preparing the manuscript for publication, and my wife deserves the *Croix de Guerre* for patiently enduring while I was writing this book.

November, 1969   C. V. G.

CONTENTS

ABBREVIATIONS

A.E.F.   American Expeditionary Force; the American army in France, 1917–1918.

Anzac   Acronym for a member of the Australian-New Zealand Army Corps who saw action in France and Gallipoli, 1914–1918.

B.E.F.   British Expeditionary Force; the British forces in France, both regulars and the New Armies, 1914–1918.

C.E.F.   Canadian Expeditionary Force; the Canadian forces in France.

R.A.M.C.   Royal Army Medical Corps; the medical branch of the British army (known to the common soldier as "Rob All My Comrades").

R.A.S.C.   Royal Army Service Corps; the supply and transport section of the British forces.

R.F.A.   Royal Field Artillery.

Y.M.C.A.   Young Men's Christian Association; responsible for the American soldier's recreational and post-exchange services in France.

AMERICAN WAR NARRATIVES
1917-1918

Introduction

Graphic descriptions of rats feeding on bloated, yellowed corpses are not charming, but the personal war narratives studied in this work would be a valid object of scholarly interest if all that they showed were a vivid picture of life at the Front during World War I. They are, however, of far more value. These records of combat and suffering in France and on the other fronts provide invaluable source material for the study of the American popular mind and its common beliefs and prejudices, and provide the background necessary for understanding the revolt of the Lost Generation during the Twenties.

Social and cultural historians have largely neglected the rich source material of the personal war narratives, although these volumes provide a deeply revealing look into what constituted the social, religious and political beliefs of the "Old Gang" against whom Hemingway, Dos Passos, E. E. Cummings and others rebelled.

The Twenties were a time of newly found sophistication and experimentation, but the period that preceded these years was one of innocence and isolation. It would be an understatement to say that most Americans were uninformed about the machinations of European politics; they simply didn't care. The British Admiral Warrender may have been innocent when he signaled the German naval forces in Kiel Bay on June 29, 1914 (less than a month and a half before the war would begin), "Friends in past and friends for ever," but America made him look sophisticated by comparison.

Internationalism was over for Americans, for less than twenty years before the war fever of the young nation then beginning to feel its imperialistic ambitions, fanned by William Randolph Hearst of the New York *Journal* and Joseph Pulitzer of the New York *World*, burst into the flame that was the Spanish-American War. It was a "splendid little war" during which the pathetic navy of Old World (and therefore decadent) Spain was properly annihilated, but the fruits of victory proved to be bittersweet, what with the rebellion in the Philippines, and the nation was really interested in more pressing issues such as the remarkable Model T and the agitation for women's suffrage.

The country was still essentially rural, but change was coming rapidly. The Census of 1910 recorded a population of almost ninety-two million Americans, of whom 46.3 per cent lived in communities of over 2,500 people. It was still a vibrant and expanding country, with 14.7 per cent of the total population of 1910 being foreign-born. The West was being settled fast, per-capita income was steadily rising and the future for the country seemed bright, even if there were a few disturbing incidents like the Atlanta race riot of 1906. With money to be made and spectacles like Woodrow Wilson fighting for his New Freedom at home to interest one, why become involved with European problems?

Indeed, there was a faith abroad in the land that life was really improving, and that man was beginning to evolve out of his more barbaric ways. William Dean Howells could write that society was becoming less violent and not draw amused laughter, and the recent publicity given to the Muckrakers showed that meaningful reforms could be made once people became aware of problems. Americans, then still innocent of network radio, read large numbers of magazines like *Collier's*, *Cosmopolitan*, *McClure's* and the *Saturday Evening Post*, and devoured the many daily papers, benefiting from the reliable United Press and Associated Press news services. The magazines and newspapers reflected a properly shocked attitude at such inroads into decency as the New York Armory art show of 1913, but generally they spoke of progress and ignored the sputtering fuse in the dynamite of European politics. Even President Wilson, himself epitomizing American morality and naïveté, fervently wished that he could avoid foreign involvement altogether. The ironies of fate had other plans.

The almost primal innocence and isolation of America during the war years is continually underlined by the tone and romantic quality of the personal war narratives, and it is significant that the general reading public, the people who bought the narratives by the hundreds of thousands, reflected the narrators' simplistic view of war, morality, good versus bad, religion and other social and cultural factors by providing a lucrative market for the over four-hundred narratives published in America during the war years. Although Henry F. May in his *The End of American Innocence, 1912–1917* argues brilliantly that the seeds for the flowering of the social and cultural upheaval of the Twenties were planted before and during World War I, he is speaking of the intellectual avant-garde, not of those who, devoid of intellectual sophistication and cultural awareness, wrote and bought the narratives. The intellectual rebellion of the Twenties may have started by 1914, but most Americans had no idea that it was even a remote possibility, much less any thoughts of abetting it. After all, Eleanor H. Porter's *Pollyanna* was on everybody's bestseller list, so the world had to be nicely ordered, understandable and safe.

There were exceptions, of course, and some of the narrators were members of the literati and should have been more sophisticated and aware than to write with romantic tunnel vision (e.g., Arnold Bennett, Winston Churchill, Mildred Aldrich and Henry Van Dyke), but most of the narrators were common people who became involved with the war and who simply tried to record their own experiences.

So much were these narratives the result of the popular, unsophisticated viewpoint rather than of the literary or academic mind, that romanticism rather than realism or naturalism is their organizing principle. This is surprising to the person who rather innocently assumes that since Edgar Howe, Hamlin Garland, Harold Frederic, Frank Norris, Stephen Crane, Theodore Dreiser and other naturalists were widely published and well established in the years preceding World War I, their generally deterministic ideas on life and literature were tightly intertwined into the American intellectual fabric. The narratives thus illustrate vividly the long time-lag between when the avant-garde formulates certain standards and ideas and when, if ever, the general public accepts these ideas. And the narratives show that while the public was ready to read about horrors of trench warfare told with photographic realism, it also demanded that the controlling tone and approach of the works be romantic.

There is, moreover, a timeless relevancy to these narratives that transcends a brief era in American social history. After studying over four hundred of these records of personal experience, their main message became startlingly obvious to me: the encouragement of the romantic spirit is necessary to wage a successful and "popular" war, no matter how worthwhile the ends of going to war might be. It is simply easier to become involved in a war for heroic and noble ideals than for realistic and practical objectives, but it is difficult to sustain Romanticism's fevered pitch over a long period (witness Vietnam).

The personal war narratives reflect America's mood exactly and are a superb example of the convincing nature of the romantic approach. From 1914 to 1917 the war was distant and exciting for most Americans, their reactions resembling those of a schoolboy reading *Ivanhoe*; the casualty lists did not reflect the awful annihilation of American manhood as they did reflect the loss of a whole generation of Frenchmen, Englishmen, and Germans. Our part as an Ally did not begin until Congress declared war on Germany on April 6, 1917 by a vote of 373 to 50 in the House and 82 to 6 in the Senate, and General Pershing's American Expeditionary Force waited until June, 1918, to fight its first important battle at Château-Thierry. The armistice of Compiègne, November 11, 1918, ended the fighting. The romantic impulse could be sustained for this nineteen-month period—there was not time for the kind of horrible attrition to develop which led to the French army mutinies of 1917. Americans could call sauerkraut "Victory Cabbage" and German measles "Liberty Measles" and still have energy left over for a rousing Red Scare in 1919. The American penchant for romantic causes was never better seen than in the writings on World War I. We should, therefore, take these narratives for what they are—literarily undistinguished works that provide a revealing picture of American viewpoints and ideals during a period of innocence and isolation, a time before electronic sophistication could record for evening television viewers the painful reality of wars thousands of miles from home.

The nineteenth-century American historians—Parkman, Bancroft, Prescott and Motley—wrote more like American romantics rather than like objective historians. "The grand theme involved the origins of a nation (preferably, in some way, American), the progress of Liberty in her battle against Absolutism, the conquest of a continent, or all of these."[1] American war narrators, 1914–1918, made the "progress of Liberty" theme the vortex of their romantic maelstrom, and produced works that were the progeny of nineteenth-century American romanticism, rather than the offspring of twentieth-century realism and naturalism.

Their putteed legs, high collars, and trench helmets in the old sepia photographs look strange now; in the dated and doughty narratives the pasteboard figures fix bayonets, mouth patriotic clichés, and melodramatically vault "over the top," either "going West" or to "Blighty." It was "a world so foreign, so seemingly simple, that we sometimes tend, foolishly enough, to find it comical,"[2] but we must not kneel to a sophisticated impulse and cynically laugh; they meant it. Shaken by a certain sense of horror mixed with admiration, the modern reader realizes that much of this writing was not phony patriotism, dashed off to help sell Liberty Bonds, but that the narrators believed in the romanticism that they wrote, and many of the eighty-three thousand American dead[3] had died believing in it. Faith, not merely discipline, provided verve and tenacity for the Canadian Expeditionary Force (C.E.F.), and later would bolster the ranks of the American Expeditionary Force (A.E.F.): "At the beginning of the battle of Ypres our lines were a little over twelve thousand strong, and after six days and nights of fighting there remained two thousand of us standing."[4]

For today's reader, cynical after Versailles, Munich, World War II, Korea, Vietnam, and the Cold War, the literary documents of World War I cannot be understood sympathetically unless one somehow is able to transcend time and space to be a part of it all. An emotional act cannot entirely be understood by an intellectual process. Only by some strange process of empathy can one today understand how or why English officers refused to carry weapons in order to lead a charge armed only with a swagger stick, or appreciate how the white-gloved French officers felt when, with élan, they led their horizon blue-bloused, red-trousered infantry, en masse, into the scything German Maxims. The war signaled the death throes of that lovely, tranquil nineteenth-century romanticism, the splendid *fin de siècle* feeling of ultimate progress; August, 1914, ended the storybook kingdoms and the stately patronizing actions of European royalty. The war was a violent transition from the old romanticism to the new realism: "When all was ready, bayonets were fixed and the attack began. Flags snapping in the air, regimental bands playing 'The Marseillaise,' the officers in white gloves and twenty paces forward, they swept forward to the sound of bugles—full tilt into the massed firepower of the twentieth century."[5] Three years later a dashing West Point colonel, Douglas MacArthur, was to lead troops from the 42d ("Rainbow") Division over the top, while he carried only a swagger stick. ("It's good for morale.")

The war was, of course, primarily a European blood lust, born from a tangle of alliances as complicated and incestuous as the intermarriage of European royalty. Before one can, therefore, understand America's romantic involvement in the conflict, one must attempt to understand the European attitudes—a thing which most Americans of the period never really did, as they languished in their splendid isolationism. How can a modern American, shocked by two-hundred combat deaths a week in Vietnam, appreciate the enormity of the sacrifice? Is it meaningful to note that a whole generation of Frenchmen, Englishmen, and Germans was literally exterminated?

The modern visitor to Oxford and Cambridge looks at commemorative plaques and windows in honor of the classes of 1914–1918, killed in action "for King and Country." In the ancient dignified surroundings the names are strangely peaceful, silently recording the subalterns who died "somewhere in France," in their late teens or early twenties, possessors of posthumous "M.C.'s" or V.C.'s." A sudden horror comes with the realization of the extent of the lists. After reading hundreds of war narratives, the memory of these cenotaphs and memorial windows persists: the tradition which fills the echoing stone halls of Oxbridge and the dignity of the memorials blend together. They represent an untainted naïve world, a world that died in Flanders and Belleau Wood along with the generation of 1914 and a totality of innocence which both Europe and America would never again possess.

By 1933, F. Scott Fitzgerald had realized that this generation and its beliefs were dead. Some of his fictional characters visit the Somme battlefield:

> See that little stream—we could walk to it in two minutes. It took the British a month to walk to it—a whole empire walking very slowly, dying in front and pushing forward behind. And another empire walked very slowly backward a few inches a day, leaving the dead like a million bloody rugs. No Europeans will ever do that again in this generation.
>
> • • •
>
> . . . this western-front business couldn't be done again, not for a long time. . . . They could fight the first Marne again but not this. . . . You had to have a whole-souled sentimental equipment going back further than you could remember. You had to remember Christmas, and postcards of the Crown Prince and his fiancée, and little cafes in Valence and beer gardens in Unter der Linden and weddings at the mairie, and going to the Derby, and your grandfather's whiskers.[6]

These same old-school romantic impulses of which Fitzgerald writes so graphically, although European in this case, were continually manifested in the American society of 1914–1918, and composed the organizing principle of the vast bulk of the war narratives. Although not products of an ancient and rigid society, Americans were nevertheless caught between the romanticism of the old ideals and the reality of the new, and their romanticism was intensified by America's isolationism and reverence of qualities from the American democratic faith such as the sacred nature of individualism and faith in the progress of democracy. Wilson Ober Clough, Professor Emeritus of American Studies at the University of Wyoming, was in 1917–1918, as he terms it, a "Private, rear rank" in the A.E.F. He expresses clearly this tension between the old romanticism and the new realism when he writes that "to me, a number of W.W.I. books were moving and genuinely truthful to the experience. But we lived in a different world, less sophisticated, more naïve and idealistic, even than is possible now. Hence the necessary tension for good literature —between an older world not quite real any more and a new not yet grasped or realized."[7] He too sees romanticism in the American attitudes toward World War I, and claims that it is always present in American life:

> Each generation has its form of Romanticism, and that of today is formed in the howlings of a Ginsberg and the alley poetry which thinks itself mature because it is "disillusioned" with LIFE. Verlaine and Baudelaire did it better a century ago, with art and music in their best. My generation had the shock of unromantic war on top of baccalaureate moralizings and patriotic platitudes. I do not think the earlier were so much hypocrites as unconscious of the coming times, and hence were a kind of sleepwalkers, muttering incantations.[8]

Precisely this type of romanticism is present in the narratives of the war, either in the form of "muttering incantations" or in the shape of clearly defined shibboleths for the "cause." It is revealing, in fact, to view these narratives in terms of the criteria for American literary romanticism as established by Richard Chase and R. W. B. Lewis. The former, in his contention that American novels are not of the English "manners" variety, but are intensive emotional works concerned largely with the two common themes of the "pastoral" life or melodrama,[9] encompasses the often highly melodramatic war narratives in his definition of romantic American literature.

In *The American Adam*, Professor Lewis sees the American literary romantic experience as basically the hope of the new world in conflict with the memory of Europe. How well this expresses the attitudes of the early American observers of the war and after 1917 of the members of the A.E.F. Teddy Roosevelt called the war the "Great Adventure," and with fresh, Adamic zeal, the Americans sailed to France to straighten out the corrupted ancient political labyrinth of Europe. With the Y.M.C.A. to prevent the deflowering of the American soldiers' innocence by evil Europe (unlike Tommy Atkins, the British common soldier, the American enlisted men, the Doughboys, were issued no rum in the trenches) and pledging to make the world "safe for Democracy," America went on its romantic quest.

It is somewhat incongruous to judge the emotions of romanticism by objective standards, "For romance, after all, is woven of the emotions, especially the elemental ones of love and loyalty and fear and pain."[10] The present study, however, attempts to separate and to codify the strands of romanticism's emotional cloak, and the quest theme is an important thread. The theme is an old one, much done and overdone, as the hopeful descendants of Arthurian knights ride forth to seek the Holy Grail or one of its many thematic variations. Lloyd George rode forth on such a quest, sounding the cry for world peace (and perhaps covertly desiring a *Pax Britannia*), but it took Woodrow

Wilson to project the Grail of the great "cause" into the popular mind and to become everyman's embodiment of a 1917 knight who sought world peace as the object of his own quest.

The writers firmly adopted the theme, and the personal narratives show that the soldier-writers had no doubt as to its validity. It took Americans a long time to mount their chargers, but when they did they set forth with a Calvinistic zeal fired by years of innocent isolationism befitting a young, naïve Christian nation bent on moralizing "corrupt" Europe. America clearly represented all that was good, and the quest was to eradicate the Hun from Europe so that the good Europeans (i.e., most non-Prussians) could be uplifted by American democracy. Sergeant Empey wrote proudly: "The Lieutenant in silence opened one of the lower drawers of his desk and took from it an American flag which he solemnly draped over the war map on the wall."[11]

In common with many romantic movements, the war had religious overtones for many of the participants, and in these unsophisticated times courts would not have dreamed of questioning the government's use of God to underline its political principles. One usually fought for "God and Country," rather than just for "Country." German belt buckles were emblazoned with *Gott mit Uns*, and the narratives show that Tommy Atkins or the Doughboy was convinced that he was on God's side, which occasionally resulted in some interesting juxtapositions because "when we think of God, we think of Him in just about the same way that a Tommy in the front-line thinks of Sir Douglas Haig."[12]

The war and "doing one's bit" often become directly connected with the state of one's soul. Owen Wister, branching out from his western romanticism ("When you say that, Smile!") to propagandize the Allied war effort, noted that "some things are worse than war, and that you can pay too high a price for peace, but that you cannot pay too high for the finding and keeping of your soul."[13] The father of a Canadian lieutenant wrote in reference to his son:

> He held that it was a mistake for a writer to lay too much stress on the horrors of war. The effect was bad physiologically—it frightened the parents of the soldiers . . . but the soldier's real thoughts were concerned with other things. He was engaged in spiritual acts. He was accomplishing spiritual purposes as truly as the martyr of faith and religion. He was moved by spiritual impulses, the evocation of duty, the loyal dependence of comradeship, the spirit of sacrifice, the complete surrender of the body to the will of the soul.[14]

Owen Wister put the religious overtones of this quest on a broader basis, and analyzed the "Calamity" of the Prussian invasion in terms of the New Testament:

> But Calamity has its Pentecost. When its mighty wind rushed over Belgium and France, and its tongues of fire sat on each of them, they, too, like the apostles in the New Testament, began to speak as the Spirit gave them utterance. Their words and deeds have filled the world with a splendor the world had lost. The flesh, that has dominated our day and generation, fell away in the presence of the Spirit. I have heard Belgians bless the martyrdom and awakening of their nation. They have said: "Do not talk of our sufferings; talk of our glory. We have found ourselves."[15]

The "glory" of this crusade was to give new ideals to a morally stagnant world, a belief akin to the chivalric romantic idea that a quest would morally and spiritually purify the knight. The war gave new hope to those individuals of 1914 who felt that the moral fiber of Western civilization was in a state of atrophy. Lieutenant Dawson wrote, "Today ideals have come back to their place in our vocabulary. We have forgotten that we ever had ambitions, but at this moment men are drowning for ideals in the mud of Flanders."[16] While a modern historian can argue that "perhaps the most important victim of war was practical idealism, that loosely formulated set of assumptions on which Americans had come to depend so heavily,"[17] the narratives' authors seem to be completely unaware that their idealism was being victimized.

That this moral renaissance would lead to a better world was consistent with the faith in progress of American romanticism, and so death was considered as a sacrifice for moral progress rather than merely a mortal loss. " 'He [the German] was dying in vain, while the Britisher and myself [French], by our deaths, would probably contribute something toward the cause of civilization and peace.' "[18] A typical comment on this theme is made by a particularly cardboard character from a narrative by the popular novelist Dorothy Canfield Fisher. A French soldier, fictitious but "drawn from life," says:

> "When a mother gives birth to a child, she suffers, suffers horribly. Perhaps all the world is now trying to give birth to a new idea, which we have talked of, but never *felt* before; the idea that all of us, each of us, is responsible for what happens to all, to each, that we must stick together for good . . . ." He picks up his steel helmet, and looks at us with his dim, patient, indomitable smile. "It is like a little, new baby in more ways than one, that new idea. It has cost us so much agony; and it is so small, so weak, so needing all our protection . . . and then, also, because . . ." his sunken eyes are pathetic, "because it is 'alive,' because it will grow!"[19]

Also connected with the romantic quest theme of the Great War (a name which in itself is hardly dull and objective), is the act of defending outraged humanity, such as the Belgians. For example, "I do not mean to glorify war. . . . But there are two kinds of war. There's the kind that a highwayman wages when he pounces from the bushes and assaults a defenseless woman. There's the kind you wage when you go to her rescue."[20] Not surprisingly, the mass media continually reinforced this image; *Punch* frequently showed Belgium as a young woman being assaulted by the spike-helmeted Hun, while Britannia, with Union Jack shield and buckler, came to the rescue. This image was popular in America even before her entry into the war, and after her entry American recruiting posters often showed square-jawed, muscular Doughboys protecting defenseless civilians. A mark of the romantic mind is the penchant for personifying and simplifying complex problems in a single emotional image, such as the ravished young female representing France.

A narrator, for example, reports that an American civilian, Miss Ellen of Kansas, drew out her savings and went to Paris to do war work at the Y.M.C.A. (run by an "energetic, well-informed American spinster"). On returning home, she lectured the Kansas burghers on the rape of Belgium: "She smeared away the tears with her handkerchief wadded into a ball, she was obliged to stop frequently to blow her nose and catch her breath . . . . Standing there before the well-fed, well-meaning, prosperous, *safe* countrymen of hers, it all rose before her with burning vividness, and burningly she strove to set it before them."[21]

In final connection with the quest theme is the image of those who actually saw themselves as modern knights, and it is the narratives on the air war that most extend the knighthood metaphor. Often called "knights of the air," the fliers romantically felt greater affinity for the enemy fliers than for their own infantry, to the extent of entertaining and toasting shot-down enemy fliers at the officers' mess. Sergeant McConnell, an American volunteer in the *Lafayette Escadrille*, wrote that "a comrade said shortly before his death, 'I pay my part for Lafayette and Rochambeau,' and he gave the fullest measure. The old flame of chivalry burned brightly in this boy's fine and sensitive being."[22]

The infantryman was apt to see himself just as romantically as did the pilot, but thought more in terms of doing his "bit" in the quest rather than engaging in individual actions. An American volunteer in the British Expeditionary Force (B.E.F.), Sergeant-Major Guy Empey, in a narrative that mixed horror and filth with excitement and glory, wrote: "War is not a pink tea but in a worthwhile cause like ours, mud, rats, cooties, shells, wounds, or death itself, are far outweighed by the deep sense of satisfaction by the man who does his bit."[23] Private Peat, the Canadian who had to cheat to enlist because he was too thin, continued the theme with "behind Ypres today there lies four thousand five hundred of the flower of the Canadian contingent. Four thousand five hundred young men who made the extreme sacrifice for King, for Flag, for Country, for Right."[24] The romantic idea that there is a clearly cut dichotomy between right and wrong, good and bad, is both closely connected with the quest theme and commonly occurs in American romantic writings.

This dichotomy had the Allies dwelling in angelic regions, while the Central Powers roasted in Hell. Tommy Atkins and the Doughboy never contemplate problems of historical relativism when they think about who is "right": "You glance across No Man's Land and say, 'Those blighters are wrong; I'm right.' If you can believe that with all the strength of your soul and mind, you can stand anything."[25] Private Peat says firmly that "it was our strength against theirs—no, it was white man's spirit against barbarian brutality."[26]

Because the Germans were both "wrong" and "barbarous," they obviously would reject the romantic notion that warfare could be conducted cleanly and according to a form of the sporting code. The Huns might use explosive bullets and saw-toothed bayonets, but the Allies fight fairly: "The first impulse is to follow the law, 'an eye for an eye and a tooth for a tooth.' But that is not the way today of a square fighter."[27]

Neglect of the "code" either resulted in, or was caused by, barbarism, and the narratives often cast the Huns as modern pagan raiders. As any good barbarians worth their plunder, the German army becomes a conscious anti-Christ finding particular delight in despoiling sacred objects for "with malice aforethought he [the German] lands shells into the cathedral every Sunday in an effort to smash the altar."[28]

The remaining part of the right versus wrong theme of World War I romanticism centers on the narrators' penchant for dealing in character types; this was a common technique of such nineteenth-century romantic historians as George Bancroft, and World War II cartoons of an ape-like Hitler and a lizard-like Tojo illustrate the survival of this technique well into the twentieth century. An American correspondent who covered the early years of the war sees the issue quite clearly, for Americans are people "who desire to live their own lives in their own way, as the English-speaking people have done for five hundred years, without having a *verboten* sign on every street corner."[29]

Fixing the blame on one segment of the enemy population also appealed to the romantic idea of intrinsically evil villains. Owen Wister avoids an analysis of the war's complex causes by simply and neatly fixing the blame on the Prussians: "Out of the fumes there emerged three colossal shapes—the Superman, the Super-race and the Super-state: the new Trinity of German worship."[30] As the romantic writer had no difficulty in distinguishing between right and wrong, so he had no difficulty in separating the natural from the unnatural.

The American had an image of himself as a natural Adamic man, which contrasted directly with his image of the unnatural mechanistic German. Francis Huard, an expatriate American, devotes much space to discussing the German desecration of her château, reacting as if the Germans were destroying Nature herself: "The wonderful fertile fields had been shelled, polluted, and among other damning evidences of their fury, the smoking ruins of every farm house stood like spectres in the brilliant sunshine."[31] For one professional American writer living in France, Mildred Aldrich, the German invasion was a violation of Nature, as it disrupted her idyllic and rustic French version of the American agrarian myth "in the simple life I crave,—digging in the earth, living out of doors,—I expect to earn the strength of which city life and city habits were robbing me."[32] In the struggle for the natural, as in all phases of the war, the romantic glorification of the individual was central to all the writers' works.

The recorders of the combat experience made frequent use of the small, personal engagement in order to glorify the prowess of the individual as he fought the good fight for the right. There is a bittersweet quality to these combat descriptions of World War I. Granted that the war was filthy and ugly, but it was still high adventure, and it somehow became brave and romantic to live among the rats and rotting flesh.

Most of the narratives contain picturesque, romantic descriptions of personal courage and prowess. It is recorded that the Canadian Colonel Birchall threw away his revolver and led the charge "over the top" armed only with a riding crop; he was wounded seven times, and finally crawled to the German trench, where he died. Lieutenant Hankey expresses disappointment at being left out of an engagement: "Now we are at rest for a day or two before the Push. I am to be left out—in charge of carriers. Damn! I might as well be Army Service Corps. I see myself counting ration bags while the battalion is charging with fixed bayonets."[33] Another Allied lieutenant writes like an early Hemingway, saying "the Front has its own peculiar exhilaration, like big game-hunting, discovering the North Pole, or anything that's dangerous."[34] After being severely wounded, he comments that "I realize that no man can grasp the splendour of this war until he has made the trip to Blighty [England] on a stretcher."[35] Even the females found courage, for Miss Aldrich remained at her house near the Battle of the Marne and derived great pleasure from giving tea to passing "blokes" from the Yorkshire Light Infantry. Finally, even doughty academicians found physical courage when *la Belle France* was endangered: "The brother was before the war a professor of political economy. From the worn blue uniforms of both brothers swings the *croix de guerre* gloriously."[36]

In the romantic approach to personal courage, fear either does not exist or is simply ignored. "Fear, in the final analysis, is nothing but selfishness."[37] One narrator not only denies fear, but belittles the Germans in the process with "we are not frightened. No; none of us showed fear. Warfare such as this does not scare men with red blood in their veins. The Germans judge others by themselves."[38]

In addition to expressing the idea of physical courage, these narratives relate the equally romantic ideas of moral courage and the sacrificial nature of death. For, "When men die for something worthwhile, death loses all its terror. It's petering out in bed from sickness or old age that's so terrifying."[39] Empey records a reformed coward's prayer of "oh, good and merciful God, give me strength to die like a man! Deliver me from this coward's death. Give me a chance to die like my mates in the fighting line, to die fighting for my country. I ask this of thee."[40] A soldier writes of the mangled veterans:

> They've brought their visions back with them to civilian life, despite the lost arms and legs which they scarcely seem to regret; their souls still triumphed over the body and the temporal. As they hobble through the streets of London, they display the same gay courage that was theirs when at zero hour, with fifty-fifty chance of death, they hopped over the top for the attack.[41]

The chance of being maimed mattered little if the combatant could "find himself" in combat and rise to new physical and spiritual heights. One American foresees "the souls of men and women rising above their bodies, flinging them away for the sake of a cause,"[42] and a young officer in France testifies "it was atmospheric, a new air in which men breathed, producing new energies and forms of thought. Men were rediscovering themselves, their own forgotten nobilities, the latent nobilities of all men."[43] An American journalist discovered that the whole Front reflected this nobility and spirit: "We had been to the very front of the front, and it was the most cheerful, confident high-spirited place I had seen in France, or in England either."[44] Finally, the hope of dying as a hero bathed in courage and glory is often recorded as being more important in the soldier's mind than the possibility of death. This intensity of faith and dedication is the hardest of all for the modern reader, raised on Bill Mauldin and Ernie Pyle, to understand, much less to accept. The narrators, however, continually claim that such feelings of idealism were common, one claiming that she heard a veteran *poilu* say " 'and when my boys grow up, they can say to their comrades, "Papa, you know, he died on the battlefield." It will be a sort of distinction I am not likely to earn for them any other way.' And off he went. Rather fine for a man of that class [railroad worker]."[45]

With the same feelings of idealism the Adamic American went overseas and promptly formed a romantic attachment for the past as epitomized by France, becoming a 1917 Innocent Abroad, as fascinated by France as Hawthorne was by Rome. He had typically "the inclination to wallow in sentiment at the sight of ruins."[46] Most of the writers so "wallowed," from Mildred Aldrich's description of rural France to the shock of such as Empey, Dawson and Bennett over the destruction of the cathedral at Rheims.

The amateur sporting attitude that the Americans and English narrators felt toward the war provides a colorful final thread in the fabric of romanticism woven by these World War I narratives. English officers of 1914 brought their hounds to France; war, after all, was but a temporary interlude in the game of soldiering, so why not have a rousing hunt between battles? They were sportsmen, soldiering as a hobby, who delighted in foiling the militarily professional Prussians. The Americans, too, glorified in the romantic belief that an amateur, citizen-soldier could, with but a little Yankee ingenuity and faith in the "cause," defeat the well-oiled German war machine. This, of course, is an extension of the idealistic assumption that the importance and ability of the individual is primary and will triumph over malignant and mechanistic authoritarianism.

In November of 1918 that faith in the triumph of right over evil seemed well founded, but in reality it was the end of an era of honest innocence and fresh idealism. After the war you could still find ads in the *Saturday Evening Post* for the Apperson Roadaplane ($2,000 for the "Chummy Roadster") and the Educator Shoe Booklet ("Bent Bones

Make Frantic Feet"), but America had rather suddenly changed. Now it was, "How you gonna keep them down on the farm, after they've seen Paree?" and, "No one knows/ No one cares if I'm weary/ Oh how soon they forgot Château-Thierry," and the years increasingly dimmed the memory of how Americans felt about the Great War, the one to make the world safe for democracy.

Today, when disillusionment with war appears to be a popular pastime on college campuses, most students are not interested in this vast body of romantic literature, and are generally unaware of its existence. Instead, they believe that the brutal naturalism of the postwar generation reflects the actual American attitudes toward the war. Remarque's *All Quiet on the Western Front*, William March's *Company K*, Dos Passos's *Three Soldiers* and *First Encounter*, and Hemingway's *A Farewell to Arms* are certainly better known than any of the 1914–1918 narratives, and it is significant that the highly satirical antiwar play, *Oh, What A Lovely War*, ran for over two years in London and New York in the 1960's.

The temper of the times quite obviously has changed in the years since the war, and it is hard for the modern reader to believe, much less accept, the romantic attitudes of 1914–1918. It is the purpose of this book to show, however, that these narratives were not merely cheap attempts at propaganda inspired by the British "Defence of the Realm Act" or the Creel Commission in America. They provide, in fact, a sincere and meaningful evaluation of the temper of the times. Even one of those who took part in the postwar disillusionment now, in retrospect, agrees with this thesis; Laurence Stallings, a Marine veteran of the war, coauthor of *What Price Glory?* and author of *The Doughboys*, in a note to me calls the study "long overdue."

These narratives have been largely neglected by researchers, and although there have been unpublished doctoral dissertations completed on World War I literature,[47] none has adequately treated the narratives as a separate entity. An extensive annotated bibliography comprises a major part of the study, for there does not now exist such a guide.

The following two sections of the book deal in depth with the narratives of 1917–1918; many quotations are used to give the reader a sense of the tone and content of the works. These two years were chosen because they were the period during which America was a combatant and thus fully involved with the war effort. These 1917–1918 narratives reflect the period of the most intense American martial spirit, and because they record the exploits and feelings of the A.E.F., they are a good indicator of American public opinion during the period. Too, since the romantic attitudes toward the Great War in the narratives written by foreigners are in no way significantly different from those written by Americans, the inclusion of the former serves to underline, not to modify, the social and cultural attitudes found in the American war narratives.

Most of all, these narratives record that lovely buoyant optimism, the rawboned, good-natured awkwardness that characterized the Adamic American in antique Europe; it would be hard to find a clearer window through which to view the America of fifty-odd years ago.

*"Farewell, Broadway
Hello, France . . . ."*

1917

On the Western Front in 1917 the Germans retired to the Hindenburg positions, the Canadians ennobled themselves at Vimy Ridge during the battle of Arras, and Marshal Pétain squelched the French army mutinies. It was the year of the Italian retreat from Caporetto, unrestricted U-boat warfare, and the Russian revolution; the year was dark for the Allies, but it was a year which saw the entry of the United States into the war, to the intense relief of England and France.

Even before our entry into the hostilities, Americans were rejecting the old isolationist clichés and were becoming increasingly interested both in the conflict and in American "preparedness"; the *Bookman* reports that the basic military drill book, *The Plattsburg Manual*, was "in demand." Curious and adventuresome Americans were flocking abroad in ever increasing numbers, some to participate in combat and some merely to be amused: "'Visiting the front' has, indeed, become as popular a pastime among Americans in Paris as was racing at Longchamps and Auteuil before the war."[1] Some went to fight, as is recorded in this conversation between a private and a British officer:

> "What part of Canada do you come from?"
> "Out west, sir!"
> "What part of the west?"
> "Way out west, sir!"
> "An officer is asking you. Be definite."
> "Well, the State of Washington, sir."[2]

The "cause" had enough appeal in America so that by 1917, 16,000 United States citizens had enlisted in the

C.E.F. and B.E.F., and 10,000 had volunteered for active duty with the French forces.[3] Too, Americans were becoming increasingly more militant, as shown by a conversation between Herr Alfred Zimmerman and the United States ambassador to Germany. The German statesman is said to have claimed that America would not fight Germany because there were 500,000 "trained Germans" in the United States to which Ambassador Gerard replied, "but don't forget that we have 500,000 lamp-posts."[4]

Before America's official entry into the war, many narrators claimed that "real" Americans shunned neutrality and believed in the Allied cause: "But all German machinations failed to turn aside the real America from its profound belief in the eternal justice of our struggle on behalf of Democracy and Freedom."[5] Americans who volunteered to fight for assorted romantic generalities before their country was officially at war received especial praise from the combat narrators. One narrator glorifies American ambulance drivers in France with their "being infected by a finer air than any that has blown through our consciousness since John Brown's time."[6] He asks, "Too proud to fight? Not too proud to carry bed-pans and wash mud-caked, blood-marked men. Not too proud to be shot at in going where they lie."[7] Another notes "the traditions of our race," and claims that "the Allies are fighting to preserve spiritual values which make our own past great, and which alone can make our future worthy."[8] He concludes that the American volunteers in France at least partially atone for Wilson's "too proud to fight" stance:

> There is something of the ancient crusade still stirring in these bones. The race of Wendell Phillips and Whittier has representatives above ground. There was an America once that would not have stood by when its old-time companion in freedom was tasting the bayonet and the flame. Some of

that America has come down to Chapman, and Neville Hall, to Seeger, Chapin, Prince, Bonnell [all volunteers].[9]

Most of the authors of the early 1917 narratives were extremely direct in their attempts to push the United States into the war, often appealing to the patriotic pride of the American citizen. "From these carcass-strewn fields there is a cleansing wind blowing for the nations that have died . . . . America as a great nation will die, as all coward civilisations have died, unless she accepts the stigmata of sacrifice, which a divine opportunity again offers her."[10] Teddy Roosevelt, true to form and thirsting for a renewal of his past glories at San Juan Hill, was extremely vocal in his objection to American neutrality and prefaced a narrative with "as in America, so in England, a surfeit of materialism has produced a lack of spiritual purpose in the nation at large. . . . The result was a soil in which various noxious weeds flourished rankly; and of these the most noxious was professional pacifism."[11]

The once popular isolationist impulse came to be called pacifism, and Wilson's remarkably naïve act of appointing the admitted pacifist William Jennings Bryan as Secretary of State drew fire from some narrators. One writes that

Mr. Bryan and his fellow-members of the Order of the Dove and Olive-Branch would have us believe that all that is necessary in order to win a modern battle is to take the trusty target-rifle from the closet under the stairs, dump a box of cartridges into our pockets, and sally forth, whereupon the enemy, decimated by the deadliness of our fire, will be only too glad to surrender.[12]

Isolationism was becoming decidedly unpopular, and the narrative of a Californian who fought and died in the Royal Field Artillery epitomizes the new American spirit: "If I could live to see our own dear country fighting side by side with England and France—well, I wouldn't ask anything more, except the chance to get in a few licks under the Stars and Stripes."[13] Another stated it even more directly with, " 'To h—— with peace talk,' said a bright-eyed boy from Kansas City, 'while these slant-heads across the line there are enslaving French and Belgian women and children.' "[14]

On April 2, 1917, President Wilson sent his war message to Congress, and America embarked on the Great Adventure. The President's approach to the conflict was not one of practical politics, but rather one of taking up the cudgel for the defense of morality and humanity, thus reflecting the tone of the American public's emotional view of the war. His war message cast the United States as an Adamic nation, a virgin in international politics, being forced into the fight by the machinations of evil Old World Germany. The President noted "the cynical and persistent attempt to take advantage of the good nature and unsuspiciousness of the United States for the establishment of an impudent system of German espionage."[15]

The good natured detachment quickly ended for the narrators who wrote after the Declaration of War by America. "It must be Peace with Righteousness and Power,"[16] for "it remained for America to make the issue."[17] More graphic was Miss Carita Spencer, an American Red Cross worker in Belgium, when she described her feelings on seeing British Empire troops: " 'Boys, I'm from over the water too, God bless you all!' But it choked in my throat, for they came from Canada and Australia and New Zealand to give their lives for a principle, while I came from the land 'too proud to fight.' (Today, August, 1917, thank God, proudest of all to fight.)"[18]

Whereas the issue seemed to most narrators to be clearly a moral one (e.g., "The murder of one American child at sea meant more to us than the seizure of a thousand cargoes of alleged contraband."), there is occasional mention of some rather naïve political motivations: "The Monroe Doctrine could not be saved in one continent if its foundation was destroyed in another."[19] It remained for Teddy Roosevelt, however, to give to the American reading public the definitive analysis of why they were fighting. He writes in a narrative that the

> issues at stake are elemental. The free peoples of the world have banded together against tyrannous militarism and government by caste. It is not too much to say that the outcome will largely determine, for daring and liberty-loving souls, whether or not life is worth living. A Prussianized world would be as intolerable as a world ruled over by Attila or by Timur the Lame.[20]

What effect the rather esoteric allusion to "Timur the Lame" would have on the American reading public is questionable, but there can be no confusion as to the ex-President's simplistic view of the forces of good battling the forces of evil.

The literary community, too, responded enthusiastically to the American Declaration of War with a deluge of emotionalism. Miss Agnes Repplier in the *Atlantic Monthly* advocated military service to provide "the patience and endurance which Mr. William James coveted, and the readiness to serve which is rightly conceived to be the supreme test of chivalry . . . . [War is] . . . saving the soul of the child from the leprosy of materialism, from safety-worship . . . ."[21] Other American authors formed the "Vigilantes" to propagandize the war effort. Gertrude Atherton, Edwin Arlington Robinson, Mary Roberts Rinehart, George Ade and James Montgomery Flagg were among the members, and Irvin S. Cobb and Herman Hagedorn were on the executive committee. Even Vachel Lindsay was inspired to write his "Mark Twain and Joan of Arc," which includes the lines, "When Yankee soldiers reach the barricade/ Then Joan of Arc gives each the accolade."[22]

America was fully in the Great War, and the nation embarked on the "Great Adventure" with Adamic, New World zeal. Conscription was passed, and "the system worked perfectly, in the face of the efforts of some pro-Germans and pacifist editors to emphasize the sufferings and dangers of modern warfare."[23] The Regulars, grizzled, tobacco-chewing veterans of Cuba's heat and Mexico's dust, went "Over There," and on June 26, 1917, "the flower of the United States Regular Army was landed without the loss of a man."[24] On July 4, 1917, the troops of the First ("Big Red One") and Second ("Indianhead") Infantry Divisions marched through Paris to the tune of ragtime music and to the shouts of a fanatically enthusiastic crowd, the Americans' tall sunburned ranks contrasting vividly with the short, bearded French *poilus*; the Great Adventure had begun.

The narrators of 1917 continually mention their being part of a "cause" or "Holy Crusade," an idea that fits in well with the romantic conception of faith in mankind's progress. Many of these statements of faith in the "cause" are overly sentimental for modern tastes, but this attitude was characteristic of the period, for as one narrator comments about the common soldier, ". . . he is developing a strong bent for the sentimental . . . ."[25] It was a rebirth of romantic affirmation, for "romance and melodrama were once a memory—broken fragments living on of heroic ages in the past. We live no longer upon fragments and memories, we have entered ourselves upon an heroic age."[26] This attitude is shown by Conningsby Dawson, a United States citizen who fought with the Canadians, in his best-selling *Carry On*: "I am setting out on a Crusade from which it would have been impossible to withhold myself with honor."[27] A Californian sees himself as being in the middle of a romantic maelstrom; he writes to his parents that "yes, my dearest folks, we are indeed doing the world's work over here, and I am in it to the finish . . . . 'For God, for Liberty, for Honor,' the call that so many have answered, if not all from as far as I."[28] It might be possible to discuss political realities when mentioning some wars, "But in this war we had and we have no choice. We are fighting for civilisation and freedom, and we must go on till we win."[29] The same narrator records what a combat chaplain told her:

> "What is inspiring this splendid disregard of self is partly the certainty that the Cause is Right; partly, it is a hidden joy of conscience which makes them know that they would be unhappy if they were not doing their bit—and partly" (I am convinced of this too) "it is a deepening faith in the Founder of their Faith whom so many appreciate and value as never before, because they realise that even He has not shirked the very mill of suffering through which they are now passing through."[30]

The same theme of the sanctity of the "cause" is voiced by Harry E. Brittain, an American civilian who with Representative James Beck (New York) toured the Western Front and discovered that "martyrdom hallows, and where ever a man has laid down his life for the country that he loves or a cause in which he believes, or is willing to do so— for the readiness is all—that spot must be forever sacred, for it is a true Calvary . . . ."[31]

A popular facet of New World romanticism was that with the inspiration of the "cause" and a little North American ingenuity, the well-oiled German war machine could be defeated for "who started the war? The War Machine that had the preparation of half a century, or the peace-loving people who, at a day's notice, took their stand for humanity?"[32] Lieutenant Harry Butters' statement of the "cause" is unusually coherent: "I find myself a soldier

among millions of others in the great Allied Armies, fighting for all I believe to be right and civilized and humane
against a power which is evil and which threatens the
existence of all the rights we prize and the freedom
enjoy, although some of you in California as yet fail
realize it."[33]

The narrators of 1917 saw a close connection betwe
the "cause" and religion, and even the common trooper
held to be fully aware of it. A Canadian volunteer tells ho
the soldiers of the C.E.F. sang "Onward, Christian Soldier:
or "Fight the Good Fight,"[34] and Alan Seeger writes, "T
Catholic religion, idealizing, as it does, the spirit of sac
fice, has an almost universal appeal these days."[35]

This religious crusade had as a natural outgrowth tl
belief that the Great War was leading nations into a sp
itual renaissance. It would open up a New World f
spiritual growth because "Well, now we know that whe
there's a New World to be discovered we can still rise u
reincarnated into spiritual pirates. It wasn't the men
our age who were at fault, but the New World that w
lacking. Our New World is the Kingdom of Heroism, the
doors of which are flung so wide that the meanest of us
may enter."[36] And an Englishman reflects the American
public's opinion of conscientious objectors with, "German
invasion and occupation of Britain would not be too high
a price to pay for the extirpation of this national dry-rot."[37]
E. E. Cummings' poem, "I sing of Olaf glad and big," was
still fourteen years in the future.

America, the narrators hint, can expect a similar national
rejuvenation when she joins in the war effort. Arthur H.
Gleason makes romantic references to the generation of
Julia Ward Howe, and claims that even the relatively few
American young men already in France as volunteers were
setting the pattern for the resurrection of an effete, dis-

solute America. This national scouring could be accomplished by "restricting immigration; eliminating the 'hyphenates'; understanding the forces of world 'righteousness'; and preparedness."[38] Whereas many modern social critics feel that the atmosphere generated by a nation at war is hardly conducive to the freedom of creative expression, Gleason claims that a new and meaningful American art will come from "a deep nationalism, achieved by sacrifice, a reassertion of national idealism."[39]

Since these narrators praise the war as a means of spiritual rebirth, it is in keeping with their framework of romantic values that they would exalt the noble sacrifices of the soldiers. Like the "cause," the men's sacrifices are often seen as having an essentially religious aspect; for example, "Men went to their Calvary singing Tipperary, rubbish, rhymed doggerel, but their spirit was equal to that of any Christian martyr in a Roman amphitheatre."[40]

The death of an American volunteer is seen as a deliberate and noble sacrifice, since his high ideals carried him so far from home to fight for another country. The comrade of a dead American writes:

> He was with his guns and no one could have died in a nobler way . . . . He was one of the brightest, cheeriest boys I have ever known, and always the life and soul of the mess. . . . We all realised his nobility in coming to the help of another country entirely of his own free will, and understood what a big heart he had . . . .[41]

Another American writes of a dead comrade that "he died the most glorious death, and at the most glorious time of life to die, especially for him with his ideals."[42] A volunteer who left Harvard for France makes certain that American "slackers" realize that it is far better to die a soldier than to live a coward with "it is the shirkers and slackers alone in this war who are to be lamented. The tears for those who take part in it and who do not return should be sweetened by the sense that their death was the death which beyond all others they would have chosen for themselves, that they went to it without regret . . . ."[43]

When death comes to an American pilot in the famed *Lafayette Escadrille*, as it would to the majority of his comrades who volunteered to fly the frail biplanes, it is not to be lamented, for "grievous as it is to see a young and happy life cut off at the threshold of a promising career, there is compensation as well as consolation for such a fate when the fine fervor of youth, thoroughly imbued with a loyal and patriotic spirit, has won from its possessor the well-deserved plaudit of living and dying a hero."[44] For the narrator about to enter combat, death holds no terrors: "If it must come let it come in the heat of action. Why flinch? It is by far the noblest form in which death can come. It is in a sense almost a privilege to be allowed to meet it in this way. The cause is worth fighting for. If one goes it is in company with the élite of the world. *Ave atque vale!*"[45]

Seemingly oblivious to the French army mutinies of 1917, the narrators record for the American public that that same sense of happy sacrifice is felt by the French *poilu*, who is still hanging on after three years of war and saying "Now I am all a soldier, and a soldier filled with the determination to fight and to conquer, and exalted by the work that is before him. If I die, and these are the last words I am destined to write, I want them to be Vive—Vive la France!"[46] Another combatant claims that Frenchmen "immolated themselves gladly in martyrdom the most absolute and complete," for "with vehement forethoughtful gladness and determination they yielded up their lives to save their children . . . ."[47] The same narrator is so blinded by what he considers to be the romantic glory of sacrifice that he can write of the hell of Verdun, a hell that was a direct cause of mutinies: "Of the thousands who have given their lives to save this gate of France, there was not one but went to his death gallantly; gladly making the supreme sacrifice for the supreme cause."[48]

The nature of the soldiers' sacrifice was such that possible death was of secondary importance compared with what the battle might accomplish. After the Canadians attacked, "Their bodies were dead, as we understand death, but the God-given spirit was alive, and that spirit was alive, and that spirit carried the earthbound flesh forward to do its work, to avenge comrades murdered and womanhood outraged."[49] Before the whistles and Very flares called him "over the top" at first light, a narrator mused to the effect that "I am glad to be going in the first wave. If you are in this thing at all it is best to be in to the limit. And this is the supreme experience."[50] Before an American aviator died in the fiery crash of his biplane, he wrote "to die, rather than betray the cause of right and justice, this is not to die, but to become immortal."[51]

With great regularity the narratives record that death is the ultimate promotion for a soldier, and they effuse the rise to glory in an often maudlin manner. John Beith records in his best-seller the first death in his company of Argyll and Sutherland Highlanders: "and so, three days later, the simple soul of Twenty-seven fifty-four Carmichael, 'A' Company, was transferred, on promotion, to another company—the great Company of Happy Warriors who walk the Elysian Fields."[52] An important factor to be considered by a romantic public was not merely that the soldier had died, but how he died; to die in "bad form" was nearly as bad as living a cowardly life. "To die is unimportant and common to all, the only important thing is the manner of our leaving."[53] An American in the B.E.F. was sad when informed of the death of a friend, "but no doubt he died like a gentleman."[54] An eager American public thrilled to this "death be damned" attitude as it once did to the dime novels of Ned Buntline: "So they have the merriest of times while they can, and when the governess, Death, summons them to bed, they obey her with unsurprised quietness. It sends the mercury of one's optimism rising to see the way they do it."[55]

The postwar reactions of bitterness by the horribly wounded were not recorded by the 1917 narratives (although in 1916 Ellen N. LaMotte published *The Backwash of War*—a bitter and brutal collection of hospital scenes) and were generally not published until the disillusionment over the Armistice had set in; instead, one narrator could record his own feelings over being totally blinded by a German bullet as "I will be happy, happier than ever. I'm in a bed alive. Oh, God! I am grateful!"[56] The remarkable thing about the quotation is not that he is glad to be alive when most of his friends are dead, but that he is glad that he had the chance to sacrifice his eyes for his country.

The soldiers of the Central Powers are viewed as being incapable of any such lofty sentiments about sacrifice, and the romantic type-casting by the narrators is evident when they rigidly classify the "Prussian type" as evil. The Prussian, with his rigid discipline, blind obedience and autocratic ways, is in marked contrast to the heroic and democratic characteristics of the Allied soldier. The Krupp family, the German General Staff and the military caste of Prussia are often pictured as an intrinsically evil triumvirate that is responsible for the war. Too, the Germans were simply not the "race" chosen by God to fight the good fight; "Again, if the German hordes, with their iron power behind them, had had five per cent of the Anglo-Saxon sporting blood in their veins, they would have licked us long ago."[57]

Ironically, the Germans who would become so involved with Aryan racial theories twenty years later were considered by their enemies of 1917 to be members of a sub-human species, for "I will not flatter them by saying that they looked like savages, for true savages in the bush are seldom lacking whether in distinction or grace of bearing. Such air as these Germans had was a blackguard air of doltish ugliness—dull, gross, indurable."[58] Indeed, they were not innocent savages, but were basically evil and thus legitimate objects of a romantic's wrath: "We are taught that it is right, moral, and from every point of view, necessary to hate evil, and, in this 20th century, Germany is the most absolute synonym of evil that history has ever seen."[59]

Too, "the ravening horde of Germans afire with the lust of blood, conquest and plunder,"[60] reinforced their Hun image by their innovation of new means of warfare, means which the narrators considered to be ungentlemanly and unsporting. " 'Let us at least fight like gentlemen,' said the Hun, with simple dignity. 'Let us stick to legitimate military devices—the murder of women and children, and the emission of chlorine gas.' "[61]

Mildred Aldrich leaves her American audience with little doubt as to the nature of the German character: "[It was] . . . the devastation of the German occupation, with its deliberate and filthy defilement of the houses, which defies words, and will leave a blot for all time on the records of the race so vile-minded as to have achieved it."[62] It is reported that a German officer entered a Belgian hospital in search of *franc-tireurs* (snipers), but found only a senile old man. Enraged by his lack of success, "He blew the man's brains out."[63] After hearing of the rape of a young French girl by German soldiers, Francis Wilson Huard, an American, writes from her French château, ". . . peace might come again, but I could never pardon."[64] Another American relates a "typical" atrocity story, of the type that prompted Allied recruiting posters emblazoned with pictures of leering Huns with gory bayonets: "The man had been shot, the young mother with the right forearm cut off, and the body violated, the little girls violated, one of the children with his head cut off."[65]

The American public's unquestioning acceptance of these atrocity stories—regardless of their truth—showed that its emotional fervor had overpowered any critical judgment. Even now it is difficult to determine exactly which stories of German barbarism were true and which were pure fantasy. The destruction of towns and the slaughter of noncombatants is an unwanted bastard offspring of modern total war and is tragic no matter how or why it occurs, but were the bulk of the narrators justified in placing all of the blame on the Kaiser's forces? Probably not.

Walter Millis in his *Road to War: America, 1914–1917* does convincingly point out how Belgian *franc-tireurs* caused many German reprisals. Too, he claims that Ambassador Page in London swallowed and passed on all the atrocity stories that the British fed him, but it must be remembered that Millis is a disillusioned postwar historian. A more modern historian of the war[66] notes that some American journalists were appalled by the deluge of decidedly uncritical atrocity stories, and that on September 7, 1914, the *New York Times* published a most illuminating telegram. It stated that after traveling with the German army for two weeks, its authors were unable to verify even one atrocity story, and was signed by Roger Lewis, A.P.; Irvin S. Cobb, *Saturday Evening Post*; Harry Hansen, *Chicago Daily News*; James O'Donnell and John T. McCutcheon, *Chicago Tribune*. Characteristically, the public believed only what it wanted to, many being convinced that the newsmen were prisoners at Aix-la-Chapelle and were forced to sign the telegram.

Regardless of the facts, the narrators accepted the atrocity stories and used them as a springboard to launch an analysis of the German national character. They appealed to the "individualism"-worshiping American public by emphasizing that the fault of the German character lay in its penchant for blind obedience, particularly to the Prussian caste. "The German nation consists of the High Command, with its hordes of obedient slave-drivers, and the rest of the nation, which in the inner chambers of the High Command is referred to as the mob—*die Menge*." The German leader is a "Superman . . . imposing his ugly and mechanical philosophy upon Christendom,"[67] while the German soldier has none of the autonomy and self-respect which the romantic mind attaches to American individualism. A turncoat German soldier writes that "we, the 'German citizens in uniform,' must not have an opinion of our own, must have not thoughts of our own . . . ."[68]

Even nature recoiled at the sight of the Teutonic invasion, or so the narrators claim in order to strengthen their case for portraying Germans as nineteenth-century theatrical villains. One report records that after a chlorine gas attack "the whole country bleached out to a light yellow and the lovely springtime spoiled—which is the Boche all over—no eye for the beauties of Nature at all."[69] A romantic attachment to Nature, apparently, was not inherent in the *Kultur* of 1917.

In addition to being natural, the Allied armies are pictured as embodying the essence of democracy, "a great democratic army, drilling to fight so that this may be a decent world to live in."[70] Narrators thrilled to the American volunteers who enacted American democracy abroad; there were "millionaires and an impersonator, Harvard,

Dartmouth, Tech, Columbia, Fordham, Michigan, Princeton, Cornell and Yale men, ranchers, lawyers, and newspaper men—all are hard at work on terms of exact
equality."[71] The democratic Allied armies were composed
of valiant individuals, men who proved to the narrators
that their faith in the prowess of the individual was justified, and there are many enthusiastic descriptions of valor
during small-unit actions.

Manliness is an integral part of this cult of the individual,
and in the letters home the strained phrases attest to the
soldier-narrators' preoccupation with proving their manhood. One writes, "Whatever happens, I know you will be
glad to remember that at a great crisis I tried to play the
man, however small my qualifications."[72] An American
volunteer reassures his parents with "be sure that I shall
play the part well for I was never in better health nor felt
my manhood more keenly."[73]

Other narrators praise the life of the combat soldier as
being beneficial both to his manliness and to his general
health, the descriptions resembling the paeans sung to the
glorious outdoor life in the American West. The hazards
of combat were minor, because "for the first time in their
little lives they will learn the meaning of discipline, and
fresh air, and esprit de corps."[74] It is hard for us with our
cynical modern values to appreciate that a man who after
experiencing the horrors of combat could still remain romantic enough in his attitude toward war to write that
"there's something splendid and exhilarating in going forward among bursting shells—we, who have done all that,
know that when the guns have ceased to roar our blood
will grow more sluggish and we'll never be such men
again."[75] He adds, "The great uplifting thought is that we
have proved ourselves men. In our death we set a standard
which in ordinary life we could never have followed."[76]

This aura of manliness so pervades many of the narratives that the soldiers' life seems to be little more than an extended hunting trip, complete with all the joys of roughing it. ". . . we will never think without fondness of the luxury it was in these days of strenuous toil and robust health to lie down after a night's watch, in the straw covered cellar bottom of our ruined château."[77] The filth and soul-draining fatigue of war are approached by the narrators as a challenge, and they tacitly question the reader, "Are you man enough to try it?" Sergeant-Major Empey says "just try to sleep with a belt full of ammunition around you, your rifle bolt biting into your ribs, entrenching tool handle sticking into the small of your back . . . with 'cooties' boring for oil in your arm pits . . . ."[78] Was the reader man enough to wield a weapon like this? "It is about two feet long, thin at one end, and very thick at the other. The thick end is studded with sharp steel spikes, while through the center of the club there is a nine-inch lead bar . . . ."[79] There is a casual and jocular manner in which the rotting or petrified corpses are regarded, as if manliness were in direct proportion to callousness. It is humorously reported that Tommies used to strike matches on the dried bald head of a half-buried soldier,[80] and a French officer presents this bit of macabre humor: "One of my *poilus* hung his canteen to a foot that was projecting over the wall; the others laughed and followed his example. The true French spirit was to the fore—an extreme adaptability, and above all, good humor."[81]

The bulk of the soldiers with attitudes such as these were basically civilians, not Regulars, and among the American volunteers there is a youthful freshness to their often courageous activities. The vigorous American is seen by English narrators as being cast from the same mold as were the men of the Anzac, as this interview with Lord

Northcliffe indicates: " 'If any one asks you what sort of a time the Americans are having, just hand them out one good home-word—"Bully." ' "[82] Who could better represent the New World than an American baseball player? "The bombing-school at Etaples will not soon forget the American baseball player who threw a bomb seventy yards."[83]

Connected with this general theme of the romance of manliness, sang-froid and courage are the narrators' tales of heroic personal actions, gallant deaths and medals for valor. One combatant recalls how a Scottish lieutenant won the Victoria Cross for singlehandedly destroying a German machine-gun nest, although he was killed in the action. "In the left-hand breast pocket of Angus's tunic they found his last letter to his father. Two German machine-gun bullets had passed through it."[84] The riddled letter and the Victoria Cross were sent home to Scotland.

At times, it is hard for the reader to decide if an act was prompted by courage or by sheer boredom; a case in point concerns two young troopers who tested their new trench helmets by sticking their heads over the parapet— fortunately, the steel helmets worked.[85] As one narrator comments, "Death, when he makes the mistake of raiding your premise every day, loses most of his terrors and becomes a bit of a bore."[86] The following quotation is a fitting summary of the 1917 narrators' attitudes toward individual manliness and courage, for it shows the type of enthusiasm that was so much admired: "And then, with a dramatic wave of his bleeding stump which sent its hastily applied field dressing flying off into the gloom, this hanger-on of low *cafés* began to sing, with immense fire and verve, the first lines of the 'Marseillaise!' "[87]

Individual courage and enthusiasm when taken collectively become *esprit de corps* and patriotism, and the soldier-narrators of 1917 often romanticized this aspect of the Great War. Tommies going into the bloodbath of the Somme battles to fight in bottomless mud to gain a few insignificant yards were said to be "rollicking lads."[88] It was written that "to be British is a great thing, and I'm proud to think that I'm going to fight for my country."[89] Could any "real" American, reading this, ignore the challenge and do any less for his own country?

The narrators of 1917 had as yet suffered no dilillusionment, and write of pride in the regiment as the most romantic embodiment of *esprit de corps*. It is reported that an amputee from the Irish Rifles told his nurse that "it's not the pain, sister, that troubles me, but you see, with a wooden leg I can never go back again to the old regiment."[90] A French combatant tells with a glow of pride how after a battle his comrades were allowed to present arms before their regimental flag (*le drapeau*): "Yes, indeed, and it was sublime . . . . Every man of all the mud-smeared ranks felt that his very soul was wrapped in the glory of that sacred emblem for which he had suffered so much and so willingly."[91] Another writes on the same theme and hurls some barbs at any Americans who still chose to remain neutral:

> . . . but even the new recruits, who were already a little corrupted—no more than superficially, however—by disgusting, anti-military claptrap, . . . suddenly recovered their senses and were exalted at the sound of the German guns. All were united, resolute, disciplined, sobered, and dreaming of having a flag on their return.[92]

Although they glorified the romance of *esprit de corps*, the narrators were careful to maintain that, far from having a militaristic and dehumanizing influence on the soldier, the war gave soldiers a never to be repeated chance for personal spiritual uplift. So deliberate is the narrators' effort at denying the war's corrosive effects on the soldier's character and soul that they often appear to be trying to convince themselves of the validity of their own thesis. A veteran, for example, writes of his comrades: "They are not dehumanized by war; the kindliness and tenderness of their natures are unspoiled, by all their daily traffic in horror."[93]

Such comments as "war makes men and hardships breed content"[94] had to come from an era dominated by the vestiges of a romantic tradition, for one cannot imagine a modern news correspondent, seasoned by World War II, Korea and Vietnam, claiming that "the heart of the soldier is never hardened by its daily commerce with death; it is purified by pity and terror, by heroism and sacrifice, until the whole nature seems fresh annealed into a finer strength."[95] Qualities such as the adaptability and good humor of men under combat conditions are still recorded by writers today (there is even a sense of this in the unreal war world created by Joseph Heller in his *Catch*-22), but the bubbling enthusiasm for the life of the soldier is a marked characteristic of the narratives of the Great War. "The men are splendid—their cheeriness comes up bubbling whenever the occasion calls for the dumps. Certainly there are fine qualities which war, despite its unnaturalness, develops."[96]

An American volunteer presents a detailed description of why war could not have an adverse emotional effect on him:

I, who am over here for the good of my soul and the greater success of allied arms, have got to go through a number of extremely unpleasant experiences and become thoroughly familiar with all the sides that go to make up the "Romance of War"; and for me these things are good and threaten no danger to the mind, because a very few seconds after you are . . . turned sick by the sight of some uncleared remains of a late battlefield, you have forgotten about it, and while the item undoubtedly left a permanent *subjective* impression, its effect on the *objective* mind of you and on your good health and spirits is *nil*.[97]

Combat, in fact, is characterized as a definitely positive influence on the soldiers' mental and spiritual development. The uniform is seen as the "outward symbol of the lost selfishness and the cleaner honour,"[98] and the same narrator reflects that "yet, for all the damnability of what I now witness, I was never quieter in my heart. To have surrendered to an imperative self-denial brings a peace which self-seeking never brought."[99] From Flanders an American volunteer records "that never will I have an opportunity to gain so much honourable advancement for my own soul or do so much for the cause of the world's progress . . . ."[100] In the process of helping the "cause of the world's progress," the Allied soldier enjoys spiritual elevation, for "in the completeness of their surrender to a great cause they had been lifted out of themselves to a new plane of living by the transformation of their spirit."[101] Too, this inner growth is possible because of the soldiers' abiding faith in God; the spiritually worthy soldier "lays his life on the knees of his God, as he takes the field against the enemy who would destroy it—keeps his courage fast, and his heart humble."[102] So many soldiers would experience this spiritual renaissance that after the war the free world would no longer be concerned with the gross and the material; or, as a narrator with a poetic impulse puts it:

> Just these things will then seem worth while: —
> How to make Life more wondrously sweet;
> How to live with a song and a smile,
> How to lay our lives at Love's feet.[103]

In continuing this theme the narratives abound with highly romantic stories of men who were foppish or worthless in civilian life, but who, in the heat of conflict, revealed the true spiritual worth that was hiding under the veneer of their jaded previous existence. One such soldier was Second Lieutenant Septimus D'Arcy, the Bond Street fop, who found his glory by emptying his Webley revolver into four Germans before being himself mortally wounded. As is typical to these stories, he makes a dramatic dying speech: "Good-bye, Captain! Knew you'd come. Don't know much about soldiering—good sport; shan't have to carry that demmed pack again.' "[104]

Readers with a knowledge of Buchenwald and Dachau will find absurd the concept of chivalry in warfare, but the narrators of 1917 saw these spiritually redeemed soldiers as being motivated by "that secret spring of chivalry." Even though the writers were fully aware that such refinements of warfare as poisonous gas were used for the first time in the Great War, they still clung to romantic legends of knighthood and past wars, finding inspiration in "the invincible spirit of chivalry which tells every fighter in her trenches that, in offering himself in the cause of France, he gives himself to the cause of humanity, civilisation, and freedom."[105]

The Huns, however, had made "a savage onslaught upon the cherished ideals of our civilization and chivalry."[106] "Chivalry, honour, and a fair name, the ideals for which men will cheerfully die, Germany has destroyed and buried in the wreckage of Belgian homesteads."[107] Although most Germans are categorically placed outside of chivalry's realm, there is an occasional description of a Hun who has not had his chivalric sense totally atrophied by Prussianism. In one instance a British officer saved a German officer who was horribly wounded and was entangled in barbed wire. The guns stopped and another German officer came across No Man's Land to pin his own Iron Cross on the Englishman; the narrator remarks that "such an episode is true to the holiest ideals of chivalry . . . ."[108]

It is in the flying service, however, that most narrators see the finest flowering of knighthood, and the image persists after the Armistice with the making of such movies as *Lilac Time* and *The Dawn Patrol*. Today, when a cartoon-strip dog autistically battles the Red Baron for control of the skies over Pont-à-Mousson, it is funny; in 1917 it was deadly and real. The lineage from the heroes of Arthurian legends seemed to run directly to these young volunteer *beaux sabreurs*, who with their white scarves, leather helmets and "go to hell" attitudes soared over the mud and slime of the trenches. An American volunteer says of the Franco-American Flying Corps that "they brought the name of America into honor and bound their glory on their country's brows."[109] The same narrator, himself a flyer, captures the mode of fascination that drew young men into aviation when he says "this flying is much too romantic to be real modern war with all its horrors. There is something so unreal and fairy like about it which ought to be told and described by Poets, as Jason's voyage was . . . ."[110] On the death of this young narrator, the Boston *Transcript* printed: " 'It was as though Prince Rupert or Richard Plantagenet had himself stepped down from history. Chapman could never . . . suppress chivalry enough to be really politic.' "[111]

The knighthood image is carried to such an extreme that a pilot often would have two "squires" for his plane,[112] and Victor Chapman speaks of his entry into aviation as "like being made a Knight."[113] The flyers of the *Lafayette Escadrille* "carry us back to the legendary times in which everything was pure and beautiful—to the time of the Medieval Knight who ran, single-handed, with his cry of 'A la recusse!' "[114] Even the death of the "knights" is considered to be glorious, and Senator "Pitchfork Ben" Tillman of South Carolina wrote to the father of the dead *Lafayette Escadrille* pilot, Norman Prince, that "your son gave his young life in defense of what all of us know is a sacred cause. He was a twentieth century Lafayette, a modern knight errant whose statue will yet grace the capital of France. Prince? Yes, a Prince indeed—'sans peur et sans reproche.' "[115]

The chivalric air war was a fine adventure, an exciting challenge which had tremendous romantic appeal for the young. A Harvard man who proudly flew his fabric and wood aircraft emblazoned with the "Indianhead" insignia of the American volunteers writes in his narrative that "I am writing a journal of high adventure of a cleaner kind, in which all the resources in skill and cleverness of one set of men are pitted against those of another set."[116] Aviators flew into combat as if they were riding to a joust: "There is a spirit of chivalry among those who fight in the air, as both sides can testify. The air alone is their arena, and neither side will continue to combat on terra firma."[117] If, however, the Germans stopped playing the game and began shooting at pilots who had parachuted from their destroyed planes "it seemed as near the border line between legitimate warfare and cold-blooded murder as anything could well be."[118]

As the term "legitimate warfare" implies, the narrators of 1917 looked upon war as a form of sport, a game of death to be played by the rules and with a good-natured enthusiasm. An American with the British forces shows his relief in discovering that "sport" still remains in modern war:

> I read of old wars with a feeling of regret that men had lost their old primal love for dangerous sport, their naive ignorance of fear. All the brave, heroic things of life were said and done. But on those trench-mortaring days, when I watched boys playing with death with right good zest, heard their shouting and laughing as they tumbled over one an-

other in their eagerness to escape it, I was convinced of my error.[119]

This narrator had keen fun in dropping Stokes mortar shells on Fritz; the gunner, when he sent a round arching into the opposite trench, said " 'Gooten morgan, you Proosian sausage-wallopers! Tyke a bit o' that there 'ome to yer missus!' "[120]

The delights of combat enthrall this young American for "there are frequent encounters and ambuscades. This is very good sport."[121] He was killed by the "sport," as was the American who enjoyed learning "the use of the time fuse with high explosive lyddite shells or some other interesting subject intimately connected with making good Germans out of live ones."[122]

Regardless of the danger of combat, however, "there's something extraordinarily bracing about taking risks and getting away with it . . . ."[123] The sudden encounter with violent death added to the sense of sport for at least one combat narrator, and his description is so glowing that one wonders if he is trying to convince himself that his enthusiasm for war is valid. "Advancing over the ground strewn with bodies he faces in every shadow the possibility of the sudden volley at point blank that will lay him cold among them. It is a kind of adventure that the true sportsman will appreciate."[124] Life without romance and adventure was too dull even to be contemplated.

Romantics they were, and the combatants wrote in their books that war provided them with a sense of identification, for the spirit of romance which they felt was a spring of rejuvenation for their dull and dry peacetime lives. For a Harvard lawyer, "War itself was a manifestation of it [romance], gave it scope, relieved the pent-up longing for it which could not find sufficient outlets in time of peace."[125] The same writer records in another narrative:

> We were "off to the wars." to take our places in the far-flung
> battle line. Here was Romance lavishly offering gifts dearest
> to the hearts of Youth, offering them to clerks, barbers,
> tradesmen, drapers' assistants, men who never had an adven-
> ture more thrilling than a holiday excursion to the Isle of
> Man or a week of cycling in Kent.[126]

The narratives pulse with excitement when their authors
record something as simple as a line of troops; one soldier
writes on his arrival in France that "it gave me thrills all
day to see these fine men come through the dock-gates with
a steady swing. It is a magnificent contribution to any
army. It's good to think of all these men coming at their
country's call."[127] Another, effusive over the sight of an elite
British unit, says "[It was] . . . the whole division of Guards,
12,000 strong, the first pick of the whole British army. Not
a man under five feet ten inches, magnificently disci-
plined and with the unbeaten tradition of five centuries
behind them."[128] Even the decimation of the Guards in the
shambles of Flanders did not dull the keen edge of the
narrator's enthusiasm.

This sense of romantic excitement was also the primary
cause of many of the narrators' enlistments, for some of
them were more strongly motivated by these emotions than
they were by a sense of duty toward the "cause." "It is for
glory alone that I engaged,"[129] said one American, and
another records "but, in a spirit of adventure, I suppose,
I tempted myself with the possibility of assuming the increasingly popular alias, Atkins."[130] A Canadian neatly sums
up this romantic spirit when he writes "leaving to-day for
the 'Great Adventure.' "[131]

This spirit of glamour and adventure infected the young
American collegians who volunteered for duty before the
United States had declared war on Germany. Many joined
either the Harjes Formation or the American Volunteer

Motor Ambulance Corps (Norton Corps); these two groups were later combined, and E. E. Cummings writes in *The Enormous Room* of belonging to the "Norton-Harjes Corps." Their quest for adventure and romance as well as their dedication to the "cause" drew to France such men as Piatt Andrews, an ex-professor of political economy at Harvard who became the head of the United States ambulance service.[132] On meeting some of these volunteers, an American civilian was much impressed by their dash and romantic spirit; he quotes a young undergraduate as saying " 'everybody has the right spirit, and we are all working together. We are living the real army life—sleeping out of doors and eating in a barn.' "[133] Although after the war Malcolm Cowley in *Exile's Return* was to explain how a nearby shellburst was to permanently affect Harry Crosby, at the time it was a lark, and Waldo Pierce, a gentleman artist before he volunteered for duty in France, gleefully showed a narrator his shrapnel-riddled coat, for he was both excited and proud to have been in action. These adventurers looked upon their part in the war as postgraduate work, and "the boys formed 'The Harvard Club of Alsace Reconquise,' and had Harvard Alumni Dinners when the fighting eased up."[134] For Ernest Hemingway, John Dos Passos and others, the war would become a different kind of postgraduate education, one that was to profoundly affect their lives and work; the shock of reality was in the future, however, and adventure was still carrying the day.

The dreams of adventure that the narrators had upon enlisting were usually fulfilled by their combat experiences; for example, "Life in the trenches, even on the quietest of days, is full of adventure highly spiced with danger."[135] This desire for adventure could be keen enough to prompt one man to write home: "So I shall be in action and out of it again by the time you read this. Isn't it glorious, my dearest?"[136] One of the most romantic and adventurous moments of "glorious" action was the charge, and the descriptions of the narrators seem to be more indicative of the American Civil War than of a modern war with its awesome massed firepower. "The impression of strength is immense when one stands in the midst of all these glittering bayonets above which float the bright colors of our flag —the wall of steel that is holding back the enemy and will crush him when the hour strikes."[137] An American aviator writes of a similar experience when he was still an infantryman: "There is nothing like it, you float across the field, you drop, you rise again. The sack, the 325 extra rounds, the gun—have no weight."[138] Alan Seeger's dream of glory is so thoroughly romantic that it appears to be more typical of a Grand Army of the Republic veteran turned spread-eagle orator on the Fourth of July than a twentieth-century poet:

> To dream of re-entering this city as we would re-enter it has filled many a night's watch. The crest opposite us would have been carried at the point of the bayonet, our ranks would have been thinned, but the flag would still wave in the undulating line of blue and red as it winds up the hillside of the town and rolls through the antique gateway, and our officers would look never so gallant riding at the head of each battle-worn company.[139]

American readers of 1917 could thrill to a French description of a similar bayonet attack: "It was horrible but magnificent . . . . 'Fix bayonets! Forward! Forward! . . .' I had a feeling that someone was aiming at me and I emptied my revolver point-blank into the head of an *Oberleutnant* who was wearing a monocle."[140]

In their romantic tableaux the writers of 1917 continued to amplify, rather than to change, the romantic orientation of the 1914–1916 narratives. They set the stage for the

1918 narratives, in which the writers could excitedly relate for an enthusiastic American audience the deeds of numbers of their own sons and brothers. It is noteworthy that I. M. Parsons, in his *Men Who March Away*, an anthology of World War I poetry, states that by late 1916–1917 the brilliance of war's glory had faded for the poets in the oozing trenches. However, most of these poets, such as Wilfred Owen, were never widely published until after the war. In the meantime what were being published and ravenously consumed by the American reading public were the personal war narratives, overstuffed with stereotyped anachronistic themes of nineteenth-century Romanticism. America was sending her boys off on the "Great Adventure," and wanted to read, and was given, platitudes from her age of innocence, not twentieth-century reality.

*"We'll Hang the Damned Old Kaiser
To a Sour Apple Tree. . . ."*

1918

"As 1918 dawned, half in fear and half in hope, Europe looked towards America. She alone seemed to possess the key to the situation. Whether she would arrive in time to turn it was another matter."[1] The Allies were tired, and it was with sincerity mixed with jest that the Tommies chalked a final "t" on the nameplates of the A.E.F.'s "Atlas" trucks; the French were not being merely polite when they said, *"Vous venez nous sauver, vous Américains."*

The sensitive and creative soldiers in the Allied armies were by now generally embittered; Siegfried Sassoon threw his Military Cross into the Mersey River, and Robert Graves wrote in his *Good-bye to All That* that the Western Front was known as the Sausage Machine, for it consumed live men, spewed out corpses, and "remained firmly screwed in place." Such disillusioned men, however, mainly published their works after the war, and while the narratives of 1918 might show the death, filth and horror of the Front, they largely did so without an entrenched sense of bitterness.

Military matters looked bleak for the Allies, for the Germans launched their spring "peace" offensive (*Freidensturm*) at the juncture of the French and British lines. The problem was largely one of numbers, for the Russian Revolution allowed the German high command to release forty-forty divisions from the Eastern Front and to hurl them at the Allies in the Soissons area. The American forces, however, helped to tip the balance in the Allies' favor. On May 28th, the American First Infantry Division ("Big Red One") attacked at Cantigny, and on June 1st the United States Second ("Indianhead") and Third Regular Infantry

Divisions held the Germans at Château-Thierry and coun-
terattacked at Belleau Wood; the proud Third has from that
time on been known as the "Rock of the Marne."

The A.E.F. had yet to endure its ordeal by fire, but the
American narrators had no doubts about the outcome of
the war because "the Yanks are coming": "After these came
the Americans!!! Oh, it was great! A score of mounted
officers leading, with one French capitaine in the middle,
and then the band, with a drum major and all! It was too
thrilling to even put down on paper!"[2] A reporter for the
Philadelphia *Public Ledger* was intent on glorifying the
Doughboys for the American public, and his narrative shows
his enthusiasm for the Americans who were coming to
France to save Western Civilization:

> The band was pounding out that irresistible American march-
> ing ditty, "Over There!" It brought the tears to one's eyes.
> Beside us a sister ship grandly swept in, and a regimental
> band on her decks was booming forth uproariously, "Hail!
> Hail! The Gang's All Here!" No one could truthfully contro-
> vert those brazen throats on the sweet evening air.[3]

The war correspondent for the New York *Times* excitedly
proclaims "never was there such a spectacle in all history
as that of the fresh millions of free Americans flocking to
the rescue of beleaguered and exhausted Europe."[4] In continuing his encomiums for the fresh Americans, the reporter writes of Pershing's voyage to France that "there is
something of a national drama in this voyage for freedom.
It is the return of the *Mayflower*, armed."[5] It might also
be noted that some Frenchmen referred to the A.E.F. as
the Second Children's Crusade.

Youthful and eager they had come to France to the tune
of "and we won't come back/ Till it's over, Over There,"
and they were ready for anything. General Peyton C. March,

the American Chief of Staff, captured the spirit of American confidence when he proclaimed "the American makes a good soldier because he is a big, wiry, rangy man and therefore excellent physical raw material. To this he adds a mental alertness which is due to his manner of life and general education. He fights with his head."[6] By January, 1918, there were 116,000 Doughboys in France and "they were young, they were fit, they were enthusiastic. Their bodies were not scarred by year-old wounds, neither had their nerves been stretched beyond endurance by never-ending months of mud, blood and a troglodyte existence."[7] As Secretary of War Newton D. Baker commented when visiting the Front in September, 1918, and witnessing an attack, " 'The pep, ginger and joyfulness of our boys was inspiring.' "[8] Bitterness and negation were absent from the narratives, and their authors thrilled to the stories of the exploits of such as the 42nd ("Rainbow") Division, led by officers like Colonel Douglas MacArthur, who, clad in a turtle-necked sweater and an overseas cap, brandished a swagger stick while leading his men on a trench raid.

Enthusiasm for the war and its romanticism was nearly universal in America; as one narrator remarks, "I have heard of a number of my friends among the fellows— college chaps at Harvard and Hanover—and they have gone almost to a man. Indeed, everyone that I knew at all well has joined."[9] For most American young men it was a naïve adventure, and they went off singing about their beloved Garden of the World: "Oh the oak, and the ash and the weeping willow tree,/ And green grows the grass in God's Country." The songs of the A.E.F. reflect the ribald but innocent spirit of the soldiers, and "Mademoiselle from Armentières" committed physiologically amazing feats in countless bawdy verses of the song dedicated to her. There is soldierly callousness but no war weariness shown here:

> Oh, I've been wounded in this fight
> Shot at sunrise, gassed at night.
> Outside of that I feel alright
> And I ain't got weary yet.

Or here:

> Oh, the infantry, the infantry, with the dirt behind their ears,
> The infantry, the infantry, they don't get any beers.
> The cavalry, the artillery, and the goddamned engineers,
> They couldn't lick the infantry in a hundred million years.

America was alive with a remarkably naïve enthusiasm and optimism, and it was hard for her people to realize the totality of the war; for the United States it was an adventure, but Scotland sent one million men out of a total population of five million.

This pervasive sense of patriotism also affected the literary community, and its products were marked by both emotion and chauvinism.[10] One must grant, however, that the worst of the professional writing was markedly better than this dedicated but amateur effort produced under the aegis of Mars:

> Then we'll tramp, tramp, tramp, and we'll fight, fight, fight,
> For liberty and freedom, for justice, truth and right.
> We'll fight on land or water, or high up in the air,
> On mountains steep, in trenches deep, we'll fight, fight
>   anywhere;
> Till every nation, great or small, from despots shall be free
> We'll fight to make this wide, wide world safe for Democracy.[11]

Prose also reflected an overabundance of martial inspiration; E. L. Pell, for example, wrote *What Did Jesus Really Teach About War*, which includes such informative chapters as "How Would Jesus Regard a Slacker." The advertisement for the volume proclaims " 'Capital,' says Colonel Theodore Roosevelt. 'I wish every religious man could read it.' " The narratives were also a source for America's need for emotional kindling, for the war fascinated Americans as an adventuresome novelty, and they searched for any means to achieve emotional involvement. A British soldier-narrator addresses an American audience with "if you are to be an Ally, we want you to be an Ally fired with the emotions which fire Great Britain, which fire poor, shattered France. We want you to be an Ally at war not with your men, not with your money, not with your machines. NO! We want you to be an Ally at war with your hearts, at war with your inmost and uttermost *souls*."[12] The narratives both provided and inspired precisely this type of devotion and emotional involvement.

The narratives of 1918 differ little from those of 1917, with the important exception that they record for the first time the reactions of American troops in combat. The fresh Americans of the A.E.F. embarked on a Holy Crusade to save the world for democracy and righteousness, and the British, Canadians, Anzac and French echoed the American's crusading rhetoric. Typically, one combatant's narrative is dedicated "to my brothers, Gordon and Billy, who are still fighting the good fight and keeping the faith."[13]

In 1918 men still rallied to the banner that was to redeem Europe from the ravages of the Hun, and the narrators phrased the banner's call in such a way that no "real" man could refuse. An Anzac writes that "there is something in all of us that is stronger than kinship, higher than citizenship—manhood—and every one who is a man will join us in this struggle against the monster that has devoured women and children and many fair lands."[14] Readers are continually reminded of the German outrages, and one narrator claims that when the troops saw a ruined French village "laughter and talking died, and curses, mumbled through clenched teeth, took their place. The spirit of France sifted down upon us and took up its abode in our hearts."[15]

Descriptions of death and mutilation are found in the 1918 works, but like those in the narratives of 1917, they are meant to inspire rather than to terrify. An American volunteer with the C.E.F. writes that "you go up to the Line, and try to laugh, or smile at least, and swallow it down. But it's part of the game, of course, and it is a noble end which we seek out of the ruck and jetsam of death and broken men and sorrow. . . ."[16] Most narrators, however, would not even admit to questioning why they were in the "Show," but wrote that they were glad to be fighting in France, if for no other reason than to get revenge: "THEY stiffened our backs and made us fighting mad. We saw what they had done to our boys from Canada; they and their gas."[17] The same narrator develops his conception of why the men fight so willingly: " 'Tommy' keeps on because he wants, he and his, to have the right to live as they see fit in a safe and sane way. If war is the way it has to be obtained, then he will obtain it that way. So he welcomes rather than dreads an attack, since it brings him just that much nearer to his goal."[18]

An American volunteer in the Foreign Legion, less sophisticated in his statement of why he wants to fight, writes that "I would not claim that I went over there to save democracy, or anything like that. I never did like Germans, and I never met a Frenchman who was not kind to me, and what I heard about the way the Huns treated the Belgians made me sick."[19] Another American signed to fight with the British forces, but "it was not my King nor was it my Country, so I wanted my country's emblem with me when I died; for I never expected to get out of this mess alive. I always carried a large American flag with me for that purpose."[20]

Why did such Americans enlist before it really was their fight? Their reasons were as numerous as are the varieties of the romantic experience, but men often enlisted for the mere anticipated excitement of combat, and later claimed to have developed a faith in the "cause" which transcended their early thirst for adventure. One Yank volunteer writes: "They [the Germans] never could understand why Americans, such as myself, who enlisted in a spirit of adventure with not a single thought of the justice of the cause, could experience such a marked change of feeling as to regard this conflict as the most holy crusade in which a man could engage."[21] Another American, a young aviator, telling why he preceded his country in joining the fight, says "Idealism is extremes. If one desires to get the most out of the biggest God gave to get, one must plunge into it to the end of its extremes . . . . Shall it be Bourgeoisie or Romance? Shall you learn life and learn to appreciate it to its fullest or shall you not?"[22]

The American combatants' reasons for supporting the "cause" are never vague: "We were soldiers fighting for a cause—a cause clear cut and well defined—the saving of the world from a militarily mad country without a conscience."[23] For Doughboys like him the reasons for fighting are simple and romantic, and they do not require delicate political and moral judgments. Sergeant Empey, inspired by the overwhelming success of his *Over the Top* in 1917, would not admit that the righteousness of the good fight was even debatable, for "this is a war of right, therefore, it is God's war; if it were not so, America would not have unsheathed the sword, because America has fought and shall fight only on the side of Right. She could not do otherwise and be American."[24]

The soldiers of 1918 may be sensitive enough to be sickened by war ("It is war that I hate"), but an overriding patriotism and faith in the achievement of a worthy end causes the narrator to modify his first statement with "and war that I am willing to give all to end as permanently as possible, for it isn't the men that war kills, it is the mothers' hearts which it destroys, that makes it hateful to me."[25] More frequently, however, the narrators' statements on the necessity for the war and on why they enlisted are unqualified and markedly similar. An American officer in the A.E.F. writes that he is in the war because: "[I had] . . . an unquenchable feeling that a great wrong perpetrated against humanity must be avenged and that the avengers, the correctors, had better be men who felt deeply and had sacrifices to make—in order to take part in the crusade of righteousness."[26] Winston Churchill, the American novelist and a civilian observer of the war, credits even the most common American soldier with the capacity for an inspirational vision, for "Through the pall of horror and tragedy the American sees a vision; for him it is not merely a material and bloody contest of arms and men . . . . It is a world calamity, indeed, but a calamity, since it has come, to be spiritualized and utilized for the benefit of the future society of mankind."[27]

Another American narrator asserts that the *Lusitania* sinking was a direct reason for his involvement. "The dishonor to the flag is great, but it seems to me more a dishonor to manhood and humanity. I can see very little patriotism or flags or countries; it is more a struggle of mankind to defend the principles of humanity and chivalry which the Creator has handed down."[28] An Australian evokes images that would stir the emotions of any American reader of 1918 when he says

> in America or Australia there are no hospitals where lie thousands of girls too young to become mothers who have been raped. We have not hundreds of boys who will not become men. A young girl said to me, "There is a baby coming it is a Boche; when it is born I will cut its throat!" A woman

> showed me on an estaminet floor the blood-stains of her
> own baby butchered before her eyes. These were French
> women, not ours. But what if they had been? Your sister!
> Your mother! Your wife![29]

To anyone who believed a statement such as this, there
could be no doubt that the war was a "Holy Crusade."

Even after writing a grimly realistic description of trench
warfare, an American narrator retained enough faith to
write: "Looking back on the awfulness of the trenches and
the agonies of mind and body, the sacrifice seems to fade
into insignificance beside the satisfaction of having done
a bit in the great and just cause."[30] The specter of death
did not deter these true believers, for "the magnitude of
this gigantic struggle against autocracy is such that human
imagination cannot visualize it—it requires one to stand
face to face with death itself."[31] The possibility of a narrator's own death prompts him to write home that "I consider you very much, mother, but more than you, more
than myself, must I be true to the Idealism of the world.
*That is the greatest god to obey and the greatest religion
to be loyal to.*"[32]

When defending this "Idealism" Americans expressed a
sentimentality that exceeded that of the English and was
matched only by the French, and mixed patriotism into
their emotional outpourings about humanity and the
"cause."

> In the afternoon, when the patriots of Alsace, 2,000 of them,
> went and paid tribute to the statue of Strasburg, they nearly
> covered the beautiful figure with roses and lilies, but alone
> and symbolic over her heart was draped the Stars and Stripes,
> our flag, the American flag. It made one's heart beat faster
> and somehow brought a lump in one's throat.[33]

The attitudes of the American narrators of 1918 on the
moral necessity for fighting are neatly epitomized by this

American volunteer who was killed in action during aerial combat:

> The choice between America and peace and France and war; the desire to be one of them over here and to feel fully worthy of France's beauty and her people's sympathy; the desire to be able to say with pride that I have done something real in the greatest of all struggles; the horror of shirking when boys like me are dying; the thousand and one other minor reasons that turn by turn assail me stronger and harder day by day as I remain in the new world of Europe.[34]

The "Men Who Marched Away" and who wrote about it in 1918 felt neither disillusioned nor estranged from moral reality.

The raw, brawny North Americans "came over the seas to fight God's battles,"[35] and in the process came to believe that they were undergoing a religious rejuvenation and general spiritual renaissance from which they could not help but benefit. A sergeant in the London Scottish states "I believe that the war has converted more men to a true Christianity than any other force of modern times."[36] German brutality often caused Allied soldiers to strengthen their religious beliefs. "After they saw the Germans using the Belgian women the way they did, almost every man in my company took . . . a vow, and most of them kept their vows, too. And those that were religious got more so, after that."[37]

Even the troopers' characteristic cursing could be given a religious orientation by a narrator who firmly believed in the war as a spiritually beneficial experience. At Gallipoli during Winston Churchill's military fiasco, "[They were] . . . the type of men that joked with death and made curses sound to angel ears sweeter than the hymns of the soft-souled churchgoer."[38] Christian metaphors are often employed when a narrator discusses a combat fatality: "As the men of the dead officer's regiment march off, they gaze up reverently as they pass by the great Crucifix in the center of the cemetery. It is to them not only a symbol of the hope of salvation, but a symbol of the glory and majesty of a death suffered for the sake of others."[39] An American narrator who volunteered for the Norton-Harjes Corps applies the same metaphor in a different manner, exclaiming "but the spirit of France was not unlike the spirit of Christ. This child of faith and truth and right arose with the fingermarks of the beast upon her throat, her feet bleeding with many miles of retreat, her cheeks furrowed with the tears of her anguish, her breasts slashed by the merciless, lustful invader."[40]

An almost universal acceptance of Christianity has prepared the Allied soldier to unhesitatingly make the ultimate sacrifice, or so claim many narrators like this one: "The Christian fatalism at the Front destroys no man's initiative, but keeps him merry and bright, and helps him to 'do his bit.' When he shall pass from the banqueting-house of life, into the Great Unexplored, he will leave as his memorial, not a turned-down glass, but a world redeemed from tyranny and wrong."[41] The preface to a collection of narrative excerpts develops the same theme in that "the war has taught men 'how to die.' There men have lost all fear of death. They have traveled the road of the crucifixion and stood before Calvary; they have caught a glimpse of something finer, nobler, truer than their own individual existence."[42]

The auxiliary volunteers also dovetailed religion into their conception of the "cause" when they wrote their narratives, for the War to End Wars is seen as a romantic struggle to exercise the will of God. Two American Red Cross workers solemnly report "the American Church was full—men from the American Ambulance Service sat in uniform in the front rows and the church was decorated in flowers and flags. Dr. Shurtleff preached a fine sermon. He said that to lose life was to gain it, and that this war was fought that war should cease—that the world should know Christ's peace."[43]

A Y.M.C.A. worker adds manliness to the religious theme. "The time has come when before God every single man that boasts of being an American, squarely, honestly, before his God, says to Him: 'I want to do my bit. I want to do my bit for my home, for my country, for myself, and for my God."[44]

While their own sons were Over There fighting for spiritual values, American mothers could read this narrative and feel confident that their boys were being both morally and spiritually protected. That the "purity" was enforced and not self-imposed does not seem to matter because "no Army has ever taken the field more carefully guarded and protected from a moral standpoint than the present American Army."[45] The narrators studiously avoided mentioning that Major Hugh Hampton Young, the A.E.F.'s genitourinary officer, shut down the brothels in Saint-Nazaire at bayonet point and dispensed free prophylactic kits.[46] They attributed the Doughboys' remarkably low venereal disease rate of eleven new cases per year per thousand troops to such inspirational lectures by chaplains as: "You must stand up and fight every evil desire, because to give in is wrong—it is wrong toward God, toward the woman— whether she is a professional or not—it is wrong toward yourself, it is wrong toward the army, it is wrong toward everything decent in human society."[47] Medical science and military police were undoubtedly more effective.

The soldiers' firm religious belief, nevertheless, is emphasized by the narrators, and the 1918 writers continued the theme developed by their colleagues in 1917 that many soldiers underwent a spiritual apotheosis by fighting God's battles. Readers at home must have been comforted to know that Kipling's words, "But single men in barracks don't grow into plaster saints," did not apply to the "golden lads" of 1918. "Life at the Front is brutal and terrorized, for there is something great and noble at the Front which keeps life pure and sweet and the men gentle and chivalrous."[48]

Some narrators reluctantly would admit that the war was a shock to the soldiers' mental as well as physical constitution, but they would also assert that this shock was generally beneficial. A Canadian claims that "war was to make boys of twenty into men of forty in less than that number of hours, but it was to purify and sanctify them in the process."[49] The author of an A.E.F. regimental history writes: "To be a member of the 'fighting Ninth' is the greatest honor that has been vouchsafed to any fighting man. We are home with the realization that we have been through the very fires of Hell, we have been scorched, but instead of alloy, the fire but gave us the true temper and ring of steel."[50] Another American writes of how the war has helped him to transcend the mundane, it being "a wonderful experience, and, if one can live through it, will change life. I am sure now that I can never go back and go on with my own work for myself. If God wills that I do go back, I must go into service of some sort."[51] Closely tied to this belief in a moral renaissance is the idea that many soldiers go through a process of self-purification during combat. "For he has been to the edge of life and looked into the abyss, and fear has stripped from him the rags of self-adornment; and standing naked between the worlds his soul has found that it needs no beautifying but the cleansing of self-forgetfulness."[52]

Some combatants had read of the spiritual rebirth experienced by other soldiers, and hoped that it would also happen to them. An American collegian serving in the Royal Field Artillery (R.F.A.) had read "The Three Things," by Mary Shipman Andrews, one of the most prolific writers of Great War fiction, and writes home that "it is a war short story, a fine thing, by the way, wherein a young 'patrician' comes to democracy, chose fraternisation and faith in the Deity—in Flanders. Perhaps it will come to me there."[53] The author was killed at Ypres before his nineteenth birthday.

The narrators' belief in war as a spiritual cleanser encompassed the idea that the beneficial effects were not transitory, but would last after the peace, thus being a sort of spiritual bonus offer for the price of one Great Crusade. As a Harvard man who was later killed in action put it, "I don't think the new growth and breadth war gives will be lost in a reaction of apathy. I believe after the war this energy will keep on and will never be lost."[54] Alfred E. Stearns, the Principal of Phillips Academy, writes on the same theme in an introduction to a narrative: "The spiritual in human nature has risen supreme and strong above the material that so recently held sway. Youth has caught the vision of the higher values of life and with enthusiasm and unselfish devotion has answered the challenge to protect and establish these values for the youth and manhood of a later day."[55] The lasting benefit of war would be reflected in the higher values inherited by the young, and the country itself would benefit by becoming "purer" in spirit and more imaginative in outlook. An undergraduate from Harvard who flew first with the *Lafayette Escadrille* and later traded the *Escadrille's* proud "Indian Head" emblem for the markings of the American air force, claims

> so has my self-confidence grown, with the help of war—the great electrifier, that banishes all stiff conventionality and stimulates passions, imaginations, free thinking and free act-

ing, till the land of war becomes a land of living poems and poets' dreams of anything you want to make—so supple and various does war make a country.[56]

Those who fought but who were not called for the ultimate sacrifice were seen as emerging from the war as better men than they were when they entered the conflict. They were to be the vigorous leaders of a postwar world in which "those of them who come back when the war is over will have the world at their feet, indeed. Nothing will be able to stop them or to check them in their rise . . . . Self control is theirs and an infinite patience, and a dogged determination . . . ."[57] America is to gain mightily through the influence of the A.E.F. that will some day return: "I believe that Uncle Sam is going to send back to their families and communities hundreds of thousands and possibly millions of men, infinitely better qualified physically, mentally and morally for the duties of citizenship in a democracy than they were when called to the colors."[58] Indeed, "I believe that the States will come out of it more united than they have ever been, and, I hope, with the many elements, resulting from our long wide-open door of immigration, welded into a people."[59]

One American narrator found an analogy in the American Civil War, considering 1861–1865 to be the finest previous period of moral rejuvenation in America, for "it is our country, and we must fight to keep it whole and bring back the ideals, just as the North fought to keep it whole in '61. We must constantly stand and bear witness for and help such big men as Theodore Roosevelt who are our leaders."[60] A British chaplain writes what is perhaps the most romantic of all descriptions of the spiritual renaissance of a nation via the Great War:

The German sword has gone deeply into the heart of France, but it will leave not a festering wound, but a well of water

> at which mankind will drink and be refreshed. Wound the
> earth, and there springs forth water; wound France, and
> there springs forth inspiration. Trample France in the mud,
> and she comes forth pure again, passionate and free as a
> poppy blown by the summer wind.[61]

The dead that were ground by the pestle of combat were
considered to be insignificant compared to the final spiritual
product that it was hoped the mortar of war would yield.

Americans were told to honor the dead but to overlook
the extent of the casualty lists, for the dead would be the
foundation of a rejuvenated postwar democracy. "We shall
find that the war will do for America what it has been
doing for Britain—true social democracy is bound to come
forth. For in the camp the millionaire marches beside the
pauper, the university man beside the foreigner who cannot speak a word of English." Another's remark might go
well with those who are apostles of a broadly based democracy, but would probably find a decidedly cool reception
among an academic audience: "It does one's heart good
to see the way men who are Ph.D's can do regular orderly
work, and put a lot into it, and get a lot out of it . . . ."[63]

A democracy based on sound spiritual values could not
be attained without personal sacrifice, and Americans could
thrill to this sacrifice for the Christ-like King of the Belgians: "Quite tranquilly, Trésignies wrote on a slip of paper
the following words for his wife: 'Adieu, it is for the
King.' "[64] Freedom "lives while men love it sufficiently well
to die for it. We get what we deserve; and the readiness
to die for it is the price God has put on liberty."[65] The disillusioned and bitter postwar writers were to mock the idea
with their tone of cynical sophistication, but the Allied
soldier from the Sam-Browne-belted general officer to the
"raggedy-assed" private was said to believe that life, "like
Peace, is only worth retaining on certain terms, the first

of which is Honour, and the second Honour, and the third Honour."[66] A vividly specific Christian imagery often forms part of the narrators' stories of willing sacrifice:

> And when the Battle of Neuve Chapelle was raging and the wounded, whose blood was turning red the grass, looked up at Him, what thoughts must have been theirs then? Did they not feel that He was their big Brother and remember that blood had flowed from Him as from them; that pain racked Him as it racked them; and that He thought of His mother and of Nazareth as they thought of their mother and the little cottage they were never to see again.[67]

Many other narrators while not so melodramatic also write of their own Christian sacrifices which are in a sense more believable than the above because the authors, unlike the chaplain who wrote the previous quotation, were the ones who were doing the actual fighting and dying. An American who was breveted in the Royal Flying Corps and then shot down and captured introduces his narrative which deals with his incredible escape from Germany with "at any rate, if this record of my adventure should prove instrumental in sustaining others who need encouragement, I shall not feel that my sufferings were in vain."[68] An Australian, himself severely wounded amid the infernal heat and flies of Gallipoli, claims that "Never were there such stirring times as these . . . . Never before did so many men live nobly or die bravely. The young knights from many lands are seeking the Holy Grail, and finding it in forgetfulness of self and in sacrifice for their fellows."[69] He continues, "Oh! What chances the men of earth have today to be as God! The highest conception any religion has given us of God is that He is the one that would sacrifice Himself . . . ."[70]

A French civilian nurse, who was a close friend of one of the most popular American narrators, Mildred Aldrich, uses natural images in portraying her romance with the sacrificial dead. "Now the setting sun stains the sky with crimson, and forms, with bands of azure and of white, an immense standard which it spreads like a winding-sheet over those glorious heroes who have entered upon the eternal life."[71] An American, however, out-romanticizes even this twentieth-century "Graveyard School" prose sample by writing

> it is a lovely, quiet place outside the wall of an old French burying-place. Far off to the West were the blue, blue hills that are on the other side of Rouen, and nearer a long double row of black poplars. And near were the rows and rows of others who had given their all and gone on before. One could almost feel a welcoming stir as we laid our first American among them.[72]

A soldier who was wounded received these remarkable words of comfort from one narrator: "But as I looked into his face and saw the look of personal victory over physical pain, I gripped him by the hand and said: My good man, when you go back home to Canada, back to your home, you need not tell them that you love your country, that you love your home, that you love your God—just show them your scars."[73] The soldier's answer is unfortunately not recorded.

Ideally, assurances of spiritual reward for sacrifice were meant to comfort the maimed and the parents of the dead: " 'Out there' bodies are shattered, but their souls are coming to great heights, for through their sacrifices and suffering men are learning the road to the cross."[74] Another American narrator, even more encouraging, offers

> and, after all, that is what America must learn to do, to get beyond, and to see beyond, the wounds, into the soul of the boy; to see beyond the blinded eyes, the scarred faces. The legless and armless lads, into the glory of their new-born souls, for no boy goes through the hell of fire and suffering and wounds that he does not come out newborn.[75]

Such a statement of faith is so positive and dogmatic that a postwar reaction of cynicism had to be expected.

These espousals of the ceremonial nature of death often embrace such common romantic images as "mother"; for example, "While it would be a bitter blow, what more could a real mother ask than to be the mother of a real man?"[76] Embracing such romantic ideals, the same American narrator is able to rationalize the death of his Maple Leaf comrades in a particularly bloody "show" in Flanders. "We are sorry. They were good boys, good pals, good soldiers. But with our sorrow is a tinge of gladness, for we know that some of those who have 'gone West' are happy at last, and that we have done a good day's work toward helping to bring the end of the war so much nearer."[77] Modern historians, such as Leon Wolff in his *In Flanders Fields*, claim that the campaigns which brought an end to the lives of Smith's comrades were senseless slaughter which did not "bring the end of the war so much nearer," but other 1918 narrators shared Smith's romantic faith in the positive nature of the soldiers' sacrifice. An American, writing of the Somme battles against which Robert Graves and Siegfried Sassoon reacted so violently, says "it is as if a great river must be bridged by building a causeway of human bodies to allow those that come after to cross in safety."[78] It had to be a Holy War, ennobled with high phrases about the beauty of sacrifice, to have the London Scottish do this and still retain their morale and *esprit de corps*: "We had but a scant eight hundred left from our battalion of nearly four thousand! There is roll-call after a battle [Lille]. Thirty-two hundred names were called out with no answer."[79]

The members of the A.E.F. were said to be as firm in their beliefs about the necessity for sacrifice as were their Canadian neighbors. The letters of one Doughboy reflect a carefully measured but firm outlook: "There are quite a few, who are varsity men, and one of my chums, who is an old West Pointer. Like me, they would rather die in France than see the Hun on top—and, believe me, we're all terribly anxious to live for we're young and life is promising."[80] Floyd Gibbons, who delights in telling how he lost an eye at Belleau Wood where he served with the Marine Brigade of the Second United States Infantry Division, writes of the A.E.F. that "I found a perfect willingness on their part to meet the unknown—to march on to the sacrifice with the feeling that if the loss of their life would help bring about a greater prosecution of the war by our country, then they would not have died in vain."[81] A young American who was soon to die in action writes home on the subject of his own mortality, "Even if I don't come back, it is all right, Mother, for you know we can't hope to gain such wonderful ends without paying big prices, and it is not right to shirk payment."[82]

It was common to write the "last" letter home before going "over the top," to be mailed in case the writer went West. The following is an American's and it reflects his firm belief in the validity of sacrifice:

> We are going up to an attack in a short time, and I am going to leave this note to be sent to you in case by God's will this is to be my final work. I have made my Communion, and go with a light heart and a determination to do all that I possibly can to help in this fight against evil, for God and humanity.[83]

The letter was mailed. Too, there was a certain bravado about the facing of death, and often the thrill of taking the risk made the price worthwhile. For an American pilot "the very danger of it impassions you. Your head rings with the constant humming of the wings of death until, superbly mad, you strain your feverish lips towards Death, the queen, and beg of her a kiss."[84] It is just this love of bravado that could inspire a narrator to write, after witnessing the

United States Marines charge through the nearly impene-
trable forest of Belleau Wood (and suffer 64 per cent
casualties), "I never saw men charge to their death with
finer spirit."[85]

After the price was paid and the sacrifice made, nature
could be counted on to provide proper honors, this belief
neatly combining the romantic's love of sacrifice with his
adoration of nature. The following passage in its sheer
sylvan imagery rivals the death of Leatherstocking: "Nature
has done all that could be required or wished for. A quilt
of wild-flowers covers this humble resting-place, and red
poppies and blue cornflowers nestle around the little cross,
and with every breath of wind nod and point to the words,
'Dead on the Field of Honor.' "[86] Nature was a prime tenet
of the 1918 narrators' romanticism, and the most natural
of all the fighting men was the Doughboy, fresh from the
Garden of the World.

An Englishman shows his admiration for the rugged
A.E.F. when he writes for his American readers, "I imagine
that your American troops will be particularly successful
at trench-raid work. I am sure that they will far outshine
Fritz, who is a methodical being and little given to individual
thought."[87] An American auxiliary volunteer proudly writes
that "I was proud to hear—what of course I knew must be
true—that our boys are fearless fighters, and that the
French consider them much like the Canadians."[88] Another
emphasizes this untapped strength from the New World
with "and so it is with the whole American army in France—
it always has singing in its soul, and courage, and manliness, and daring, and hope. That kind of an army can never
be defeated. And no army in the world, and no power, can
stand long before that kind of an army."[89]

Too, American democracy was to be strengthened on the
battlefields of France, for "here in this hospital ward was

the new melting pot of America. . . . The wounded are the real and the new Americans—born in the hell of battle."[90] A correspondent wrote of the 77th ("Liberty") Division from the "melting-pot" area of New York City's Lower East Side:

> For swagger, for snap . . . for dash and spunk and deviltry in the fighting . . . our army can show no better soldiers . . . . They are the foreign-born Jews and Italians and Slavs of New York's East Side, that were called up for service in the first draft. No wonder the mother who didn't raise her boy to be a soldier has become an extinct species back home.[91]

If 1918 showed, however, the splendidness of the American national character, it reinforced the narrators' conviction that the Germans were intrinsically evil.

By 1918 the narrators obviously felt that lurid stories of German atrocities had already been given sufficient coverage, so they did not concentrate on them as much as did the narrators of the earlier years. One American is moved to some rather inspired diction when he calls the Germans "precocious degenerates" who do things that are "simply fiendish,"[92] and two American girls hint darkly at necrophilia. "This destroying graves has also had a very infuriating effect on the people in the district, particularly as there are such awful stories afoot about the Germans using their dead for all sorts of horrible purposes."[93] The narrative goes on to insinuate that such perversions are the unnatural result of a people following a militant autocracy rather than a democracy.

The writers were quick to type the German national character, and often mentioned the German people's supposed love of order as an unenviable contrast to the Anglo-Franco-American traits of spontaneity and resourcefulness. An Australian writes, "The god of the German is *Method*, and his goddess *System*. . . ."[94] An American who was imprisoned by the Germans derides the Hun by laughing at his rigid discipline: "Fritz is like some other hot sketches—he is funniest when he does not mean to be. Every German is a vaudeville skit when he acts natural."[95]

The above is mild, however, compared to the remarks on German "brutality." One combatant sees the *Boche* as "brute beasts in the eyes of all humanity,"[96] and another combines the German "traits" of methodical planning and brutality, attesting that "the German Government made savagery, brutality, and bestiality a deliberate policy, and now it is their unconscious impulse."[97] A Canadian is vivid with "the bestiality of the Hun has descended to such depths of infamy that it is impossible quite to class them with any other breed of vermins; it would be an insult even to the rat."[98] Even German women are excluded from the humanistic virtues of Western civilization because "it is the common, middle-class German women who delight in holding a cup of water to the parched lips of a wounded Ally prisoner, only to dash it away and spit in his face in derision."[99] This comment is noteworthy because it blames the entire German nation, not just the Prussians, who were singled out for abuse by the earlier narrators. Another narrator refuses to differentiate between Germans, commenting with acerbity that "to the German Eagle every living creature is legitimate prey. No blood upon the lintel can save the inmate; not even the cross of blood on the hospital tent or ship. Wounded or whole, combatant or noncombatant, its beak and talons tear the tender flesh of all and its lust is not sated."[100] Regarding the combat prowess of the common German soldier, "His arm is not steeled by the cry of humanity nor by the cries of murdered women and children."[101]

The supposed murdering of noncombatants by Germans is frequently referred to, and a Scottish soldier claims that he actually saw Belgian children with their tongues and hands amputated. An English officer writes of interviewing Belgian women, reporting

> some had lost their children and they told how the poor little innocent victims had been carried on bayonets by the savage brutes of soldiers. Others gave ghastly accounts of how the wretched women had been maltreated, how some had their breasts cut off and nailed to doors, as a warning of what would happen to any one who dared oppose the will of the invader.[102]

If stories of perversity and mutilation were not enough to inflame the morally indignant reader, the story of a mad German physician might; it is recorded that a group of "grinning Teuton soldiers" watched while a Hun doctor cut all of the tendons of a prisoner's hand and removed the bone of the middle finger "on purpose."[103] No description of German barbarism, however, could be more forceful and shocking than this description of how the Hun had outraged nature, God and womanhood: "It was the nude body of the Mother Superior. . . . She had been nailed to the door. She had been crucified."[104]

In contrast, it is worth noting that the German personal war narratives accuse the Allies of similar atrocities; the famous "Red Baron," Manfred Freiberr von Richthofen, writes "French cuirassiers had issued from the forest in order to plunder the fallen horses and the brave Uhlans."[105] The translation of the Baron's narrative was published with stern warnings to Americans that it was full of propagandistic untruths.

Anti-German comments were not, however, considered to be propaganda in 1918, and the narrators appear to be competing to see who could describe the most ingeniously barbaric incident of German horror. A German U-boat commander is accused of ordering survivors' lifeboats to link together so that he could tow them "toward land," and then diving and taking the small boats with him.[106] The most notorious of all these tales is reported by several narrators (but discounted by Robert Graves) and concerns the crucifixion of a captured Canadian sergeant. He allegedly was raised on his cross above the German trench directly in the line of Canadian fire. In light of such events, the narrators consider Allied retaliation as just, proper and in no way barbarous. The Hun used "cowardly methods," such as feigning a wound and then bayoneting his captor in the back, "So the Senegalese, who are marvellous with the knife, cut the throat. It is the only safe method."[107] A Canadian is reported to have told a German who raised his hands in surrender that "when mercy is yours to give, you never give it. You cut my pal's throat like some porker. . . . Mercy? Hell! With that the bayonets in our hands got busy, and there were five less Germans to wear the Iron Cross that night."[108]

There are exceptions to this spirit of vengeful hatred toward the Germans; a Yankee combatant writes of the butchery of war, but writes without the postwar tone of tired bitterness. "I think the sight of those war-torn boys, haggard and hard, already touched with cruelty and blood lust, brought home to me closer than ever before what a hellish thing war is, and how keenly Germany must be suffering, along with the rest of us."[109] Still, the same narrator states that he wrote his narrative to awake America to the "dangers of Prussianism," so that the "cause" must have still had meaning for him.

The desire for Allied troops to avenge German atrocities is often used by the narrators as a means of leading into a discussion of the fine virility, courage and *esprit de corps* of the Tommies, *poilus* and Doughboys. A Belgian officer writes in praise of his troops that "everyone is acquainted with our *diables noirs* . . . that band of brave men who always set out laughing, dressed their wounds whilst singing, and returned to the fight the following day, their natural ardour increased by the desire to avenge the deaths of the previous day."[110] An American doctor on the Russian front is quick to speak in glowing terms about the courage and dedication of the Russian troops (before the Revolution) in sacrificing themselves because the Russian army was so ill equipped. "These men simply could not be downed. They would sit in the trenches and be blown to pieces— regiment after regiment—when they did not have the shells to reply to the Germans."[111] Today's reader tends to think in terms of the resulting troop mutinies, rather than about the romance of simple peasant loyalty.

The theme of soldierly courage is continued in the 1918 narratives in much the same way that it was presented in 1917, with the emphasis being on the individual as a strong independent figure. One American volunteer asserts his own manhood with "I do not mind saying that I was glad whenever I slipped my bayonet into a Turk, and more glad when I saw another one coming."[112] The same narrator does describe the gruesome horrors of trench warfare, but implies that it is a test of one's manhood to see it through: "He was an awful mess. The veins were sticking out of his neck, and one side of him was blown off, so you could see his entrails."[113] Such experiences did not embitter him, however, and he could write admiringly that "the corporal did as pretty a bit of work as I ever saw. He jumped for the boche who had fallen, landed on his face with both feet, and gave it to the next one with his bayonet all at the same time."[114]

Tales of prowess and valor are common in the combatants' narratives of 1918, for as one writer gleefully recalls, "The Great War discloses feats of valor with which nothing can compare that comes out of the mist of 'days of old when knights were bold.' "[115] The same narrator sees nothing unchivalrous in the trapping of Germans like possums in a tree. "We finally got them; not a single baby killer escaped; it was a case of getting limburgers in an apple tree."[116] So physically courageous and firm in their beliefs were the Allied soldiers that "he parted gladly with his dented member when the O.C. told him that his grit and endurance were a splendid example for the entire unit,— 'Aye,' he added, 'and for the whole Empire.' "[117]

Lieutenant Abbey, an American in the B.E.F., received the *Manual of Prayers for Workers* from home and found much comfort in reading the Manliness section. Indeed, the desire to react to combat in "good form" and to prove manliness is at times almost an obsession with the combatants. One writes with pride, "There is something about a firing-line that tightens your sinews and lends a triple toughness to your muscles. I have seen men fight for days, uncomplaining and unfatigued."[118]

Manliness and courage often resulted in a charnel house due to the tactical nature of trench warfare and the advanced state of weaponry, but this soldier was proud of the sacrifice. During the Battle of Lille the Black Watch charged and "that day, it is estimated, the Germans had a machine-gun for every five yards of front. A machine-gun can pour out six hundred to six hundred and fifty bullets per minute. It was into this hail of steel that our friends, the Black Watch, plunged."[119] The narrator reports that none of the eight-hundred men returned. More impressive for the modern reader, however, is the manliness reflected in the quiet stoicism that a narrator might show, even after honestly admitting to his own fear.

> I experienced, too, moments of intense fear during close bombardment. I felt that if I was blown up it would be the end of all things as far as I was concerned . . . . At any rate,

one could but do one's bit, and I hoped that a higher power than all that which was around would not overlook me or any other fellows on that day.[120]

Acting in the tradition that built the Empire, the same narrator watched quietly while the two-inch-in-diameter hole in his hip was dressed, and then, "Much refreshed," he "quietly looked at a new issue of *The Tatler*."[121] An American admits with admiration that "if there is one thing that the Britisher does better than another, it is getting ready to die. He does it with a smile,—and he dies with a laugh."[122] Or he might die with quiet stoicism as when " 'A cigarette, men. I'm going west soon, and I've got to have a cigarette before I start.' "[123]

Even now it is not difficult to admire such courage, but some of the more flowery attestations to manliness and courage were anachronistic and foolish even by 1918 standards. The admiration for the type of courage shown here should have been abandoned when the British army phased out red tunics as battle dress:

> "Eton boys never duck," replied the young aristocrat. He was an Eton boy and would rather die than fall short of the Eton standard. In this war hundreds of them have died rather than save themselves by something which did not measure up to the Eton standard.
>
> If the muscles of their necks show a tendency to relax they call to mind how inflexible their fathers have stood in bygone days, and their necks become stiff and taut once more. Wellington said that Waterloo was won on the playing fields of Eton. It's still true that "Eton boys never duck" to the foe; nor do the soldiers they lead.[124]

Never ducking on the Western Front usually led to unwanted perforations, but wounds should not be unduly troublesome if one followed Sergeant Guy Empey's advice:

> If you get hit and the blood runs out,
>> Don't cry and whimper from the ground,
> But FACE that trench, don't turn about,
>> Cheer, tho' it's from the Great Beyond.[125]

The British and French may have been stoical and courageous, but the narrators saw the fullest flush of youthful vigor, pride and manliness in the troops from the new dynamic nations of America and Australia, and it is in this additional material that the 1918 narratives most differ from those of 1917. An Australian trooper writes that "the Gods love romance, else why was the youngest nation of earth tried out on the oldest battlefield of history?"[126] As saviours from down under, the Anzacs came in their digger hats to fight for the "cause" and to prove both their masculine and spiritual worth; "There may be beings who could see daughter violated or brother mutilated without taking personal vengeance, but such men should not be permitted to breathe the air of MEN."[127]

A true New World figure is celebrated for showing the decadent Old World Germans the nature of Australian manliness, for "I remember that one of our men, who was champion wood-chopper of Australia before the war, drove his bayonet through a German and six inches into a hardwood beam, and as he could not withdraw it, had to unship it, leaving the German stuck up there as a souvenir of his visit."[128]

While the Aussies may have won distinction for decorating beams with impaled Germans, the Doughboys won the award for showing the most naïvéte while conducting the war with enthusiasm and vigor. America was a young country, and her men were both youthful and lacking in European sophistication. On one occasion, the Doughboys with their comically bad French pronunciation referred to the *Folies Bergères* as "Foley's Place," reputed to be a saloon

84

run by an Irishman named Foley. The French are supposedly still trying to discover how some cold but resourceful Doughboys managed to steal a red-hot, cast-iron stove from the waiting room of a train station.

A common conception was that when the fresh, brave and democratic Americans met the tired, cowardly and autocratic Germans, Fritz would not stand and fight. "As an English officer said, 'When Fritz meets the Sammies, hell will break loose.' "[129] "Sammy" (Uncle Sam), incidentally, was the sobriquet which along with "Teddies" (Theodore Roosevelt) a fanciful press tried to tie to the American soldier; calling him either to his face was an invitation to assault and battery. The soldier himself preferred "Doughboy," a corruption of "adobe," for the dust which covered United States cavalry troopers during "Black Jack" Pershing's abortive Mexican border campaign.

An A.E.F. officer enthusiastically bubbles, "All I have to say is 'Wait until our boys are in the trenches!' I also say to him that there will be a good opportunity to see whether God is as good and close a friend as their Kaiser's been claiming."[130] Another American narrator sees the Doughboys as causing severe ague in the German high command because "the German sees an American army of ten million young men, fresh men, daring men, courageous men, an army of the cleanest, finest youth of the entire civilized or uncivilized world."[131] Too, the young Americans are often pictured as breathing new life into the antique French: "Spokane Steve and Yvonne of the family of Jeanne d'Arc had launched into a discussion of prize fighting and chewing tobacco."[132] It is a pity that Spokane Steve's phrasebook French is not recorded.

America's young men in khaki uniforms and roll puttees are not only pure and courageous, but are naturally prone to willing sacrifice; because of their "normal, healthy American appetite," they are, "more concerned about getting a square meal than about losing a limb."[133] The Doughboy is of such sturdy fiber that combat neither scares nor disillusions him: "He does not need to be told that this war isn't a grinding process of attrition between the millstones of the gods. He knows that the grist that is there abrased and pulverized is the stuff of which the Lord has made the hearts of men."[134] Death itself held no fear for the American soldier as the reporter envisioned him, for the promise of a spiritual and moral renaissance overrode any fear of the possibility of death.

> No man can face death or see his comrades go to the Great Unknown, and remain unchanged. Splendid lessons of self-sacrifice are learned daily. Everything material in life has an altered value, and new spiritual influences create an idealism over the stern veneer that hardship and lack of comfort create.[135]

The writers were enthralled by the romance of the fresh soldiers from the West coming to do battle with the autocratic degenerates from central Europe; echoing Walt Whitman, their work is a romance with the people. "The sergeant remarked 'If that damned Kaiser can lick ten million of them he's going some.' Here stood six-feet-three-inches of Nebraska plowboy, blue of eye and red of cheek, flanked by Bad Hair, the pure-blooded Sioux Indian. . . ."[136] Another shows a feeling of pride over the Doughboy's rude power, for "the longer stride gives the Doughboy an uneven gait. He looks like a man walking across a plowed field and yet you cannot miss a sense of power."[137] The war was but a temporary diversion, and it was approached with a naïve and athletic enthusiasm. Upon firing the first American shot of the war, "The lieutenant smiled at the recollection of the adventure. It meant as much to him as a sixty-yard run in the Princeton game or a touchdown against Yale."[138]

These supercharged Americans are usually cast as belonging either to the "old" Yankee stoical East, or the raw powerful West. A narrator is proud of a New Englander of the type that formed the 27th ("Yankee") Division, because "He was descended from Henry Adams, of Braintree, Massachusetts, the common ancestor of Samuel Adams and John Adams; and on his mother's side from the Wilson family of Virginia, of whom one member was killed fighting at Monmouth and another fell in the War of 1812."[139] It was the Westerners, however, that best fitted the idealized conception of the Adamic American. "The Ninety-first division, which trained at Camp Lewis and includes many Oregon men, has been cited for gallant action on the field. . . . The best blood of the free West is in the veins of its young men."[140] The following description is not of the Frémont expedition, however, but of General Pershing's men in France: "The great mountains have challenged them to deeds of daring in which their manliness was developed. Most of them are unafraid, and they have been taught that there is no rightful place in the Far West for men whose blood is not red."[141] A Pacific Northwesterner, Major E. A. Powell, wrote in *Scribner's Magazine* of "the thrill of pride which runs up my spine when I see these loose-limbed, brown-faced, clear-eyed sons of the Far West go swinging by under the slanting lines of steel."[142]

These were the new men, the hope of the Allied world. When they arrived in France they contrasted vividly with the Old World, and General Pershing provided a sharp juxtaposition with the old as he delivered a speech from among the ancient buildings. The General

stood on a mound at the rear of a beautiful chateau of Norman architecture, the Château de Jard, located on the edge of the town of Chaumont-en-Vexin . . . . Birds were singing somewhere above in the dense, green foliage, and the

sunlight was filtering through the leaves of the giant trees
. . . . He referred to the opportunity then present for us, whose
fathers established liberty in the New World, now to assist
the Old World in throwing off its yoke of tyranny.[143]

The troopers were strong but green, and even their
officers reflected a fresh approach (albeit innocent) to discipline. One officer-narrator states that he dealt with his
men as "a friend and teacher," but if they did not play
"square . . . it would be necessary for me to deal with them
as an officer of the United States Army." Then, to prevent
his lambs from wandering astray, he gave a "straight talk"
on "venereal perils."[144] The narrators applauded the fact
that in the A.E.F. there was little place for the formalities
of European armies: "With an admirable lack of dignity
quite becoming a national guard cavalry major in command
of regular army artillery, he said, 'Good-night, men, we
licked hell out of them.' "[145]

The narrators of 1918 rejoiced in relating tales of the
unsapped prowess of the Americans, and one records that
"certain ones will fall surely," but "it's a man's fight."[146]
And "men" they were, as a narrator shows in these two
episodes; the first was told to him by an English-speaking
German prisoner, and the second, an extremely famous
incident, happened in the Bois de Belleau:

> "He wore his helmet far back on his head. And he did not
> have his coat on. His collar was not buttoned: it was rolled
> back and his throat was bare. His sleeves were rolled up to
> the elbow. And he had a grenade in each hand.
> "Just then he looked down the stairs and saw me—saw me,
> a major—and he shouted roughly, 'Come out of there, you
> big Dutch Bastard, or I'll spill a basketful of these on you.' "[147]

. . .

This old gunnery sergeant was a Marine veteran. His cheeks
were bronzed with the wind and the sun of the seven seas.

The service bar across his left breast showed that he had fought in the Philippines, in Santo Domingo, at the walls of Peking, and in the streets of Vera Cruz. . . .

As the minute for the advance arrived, he rose from the trees first and jumped out onto the exposed edge of the field that ran with lead, across which he and his men were to charge. Then he turned to give the charge order to the men of his platoon—his mates—the men he loved. He said: "Come on, you sons-o'Bitches! Do you want to live forever?"[148]

They were portrayed as strong men with a touch of earthy bravado, and they were also Innocents Abroad. After absorbing the "historical dope" on Orléans, a Doughboy on leave went to Paris and then wrote home that "Jimmie Clark and I sure had a good time; and I am here to say that 'Gay Paree' is some burg. It has numerous interesting and beautiful buildings, boulevards, bridges and gardens."[149]

Closely connected with the narrators' deification of the courage, manliness and Adamic qualities of the Americans is the romantic theme of chivalry that is present in the 1918 narratives. The memory of inspirational women haunts the combatants, and the cardboard creatures of their reveries appear to have been lifted directly out of a James Fenimore Cooper novel. "Their women gave them [soldiers] inspiration and joy in the days of peace, and they still float before their vision amid the blackened ruins of war, as beautiful and stainless in their purity as the white swan on the moat of Ypres."[150] Suffering can be made meaningful if one believes that "it is not the being hit with shrapnel. It is not the wound of the flesh. But it is the gnawing of one's heartstrings for the one one has left behind, the wife, the sweetheart, the mother, the sister."[151] Even the A.E.F. nurses were expected to maintain the womanhood image of the age of innocence, so "they voted to go on the water-wagon and not to smoke while they were over here. . . ."[152]

Most of the reference to chivalry by the 1918 recorders

of the war, however, dealt not with women but with the fighting men. While dining at Verdun a narrator does not think of rotting corpses in the area, but "thoughts of Knights Templar and Crusaders came to me, and there seemed something of consecration about it all."[153] The chivalric regard held by the 1917 narrators toward the intrepid airmen had not diminished, but it increased as the infantrymen became more and more frustrated by the slow progress of the ground war. Congress, in fact, was so enthralled by the well-publicized exploits of American airmen that it refused to remove their 50 per cent bonus, despite the recommendation of General Pershing who felt that it was bad for the infantryman's morale.

Two American flyers aptly describe the visions of glory which drew men to risk their lives in "Spads" and "Nieuports":

> I envied the fliers. Here was I in mud up to my knees either in the trenches or on the roads and getting very little out of war but lots of hard work. The other fellows were sailing around in the clean air while I had to duck shells all the time and run chances of being caught by the machine guns and snipers. Of course, the aviators were also being shelled, but they never seemed to get hurt.[154]

> •   •   •

> I have been at the front for the past three months now and have had so far a rather exciting and enjoyable time of it. The aviation work is so far removed from the dirt and bloodiness of ground-war, that it seems like a different existence. We have always good meals and accommodations; and our death is generally a clean one.[155]

At times, the desire to emphasize the eagle-like nature of the Allied airman resulted in a thoroughly simple-minded statement. Of Guynemer, the greatest French air ace, "Some people at Compiègne, the family home, told me that Guynemer was carefully examined when a lad for an abnormal heart, and the doctor found that the organ was singularly like a bird's."[156]

The typical flyer was held to be a cut above his "gravel-grinding" counterparts on the ground, even if the aviator were German. An American volunteer claims "the only chivalry in this war on the German side of the trenches has been displayed by the officers of the German Flying Corps."[157] On the other side, Baron von Richthofen narrates that after shooting two Englishmen down "alive," he landed next to them and "the two Englishmen . . . greeted me like sportsmen."[158] The scourge of the Royal Flying Corps, the Red Hun was finally shot down, and "we buried the remains of the Red Hun, for he had been a real sportsman. But there was little left of him. That little we gathered in a sack and the chaplain read the burial services at his grave."[159]

The flyers themselves were often portrayed in the narratives more like flamboyant cavalry officers of the Napoleonic Wars than as twentieth-century combatants. "Randy," for example, showed his good breeding by looking at the conflict as a "gentleman's war." An Oxfordian, he was "a gentleman and a sport" who would go out "just to tease the Huns": "He would fly behind the Hun lines and of course the 'Archies' would start working on him, and for every shell that 'Archie' exploded, Randy would give him a loop."[160] After his daily sport the aviator would return home and resume his reading of the Classics.

The 1918 narrators like their 1917 counterparts constructed a direct metaphorical relationship between the aviator and the knight. "There is the fire of the Old Crusader about them; they have caught the realization of the glory of humanity as they march into the face of death."[161] The mother of a killed American flyer received a letter of condolence informing her that mothers "have offered their sons, and heroically too, since time's evolution of nations first revealed to man the necessity of war. But you have been the mother of an aviator. Jack belonged to the race of aerial cavaliers. To them earth is a place of bondage, for they have tasted the thrill of the heavens."[162] A "clean" glamorous death was part of the attraction in becoming an aviator, for the casualty statistics meant little. A youthful flyer writes "In the American Field Service, the percentage of death (therefore of bravery and risk) was one-fifth, while in aviation the percentage was eighty per cent."[163] Shortly after writing this, the narrator became one of the 80 per cent.

Paralleling this theme of chivalry was the widely spread belief in "playing the game." One narrator entreats, "Didn't the British sailors rescue the drowning Germans? ' 'Tis not what you do, lad, that makes your name, but *did you play the game.*' "[164] The Germans often were enveighed against for not "playing the game," and gas warfare "was thoroughly illustrative of the Prussian idea of the game."[165] This was decidedly unsporting and, "In the prize ring, the Kaiser would have lost the decision then and there."[166] Allied sportsmanship, however, could not be condemned if it had to stoop to using German techniques in self-defense. Thus "they were to die in agonies as those Canadians had died—agonies such as no man has ever known, and we were glad that the British, who above all things likes to fight in a clean, sportsmanlike manner, had taken off the gloves and were fighting the devil with his own weapons."[167]

Although the square-heads might do things in bad form and make it unpleasant for the Allies, British flyers could always divert themselves by scaring up pheasants with airplanes, while fellow aviators stood by on the ground with shotguns ready. Death for these sportsmen was more of an abstraction than a reality, when "a few minutes later I landed two fields away from the wreck and ran over to see the kill I had made. I had hit the Hun about fifty times and had nearly cut off both his legs at the hips. . . . I carried off a piece of his prop and had a stick made of it."[168] That night the victory was celebrated with a champagne banquet. Even on the ground this sense of "playing the game" was prevalent. After returning from a trench raid during which he had bayoneted a *Boche*, an infantryman writes: "We had met our crisis and come through without flinching and with credit to ourselves [and] our battalion . . . and by good, clean, fair methods of fighting."[169]

After the United States entered the fight, the narrators delighted the American public by recording that her sons had the same "Anglo-Saxon" pride in sportsmanship as did the British. "They came over here to play the game and they have done it. . . ."[170] This New World exuberance is reflected by an ex-Pimlico jockey who discovered that killing was as much fun as horse racing when " 'we started to the machine guns and began pouring it on 'em. The minute some of 'em would start out of the town we would wither them. Holy mother, but what a beautiful murder it was.' "[171]

The motivations that led such a man to volunteer for combat were frequently analyzed by the authors of 1918, and their narratives show that while the "cause" was motivation enough for many, others flocked to the Front because it offered a combination of romance, adventure, excitement and glory. One of the more literary narrators, in fact, sees the Great War as a welcomed relief from "bourgeois" realism. He writes that "when reading *Madame Bovary* I was happy to know that I was not a bourgeois, that I was not a feeble dreamer with dreams never realized, even completed or specified, but that just outside were the beautiful birds of paradise [airplanes] which I could make lead me to real idealism. . . ."[172]

This thirst for "idealism" and excitement is still present in the British narratives of 1918, which told the American public much about the deep, almost inbred, romantic orientation of the combatants, who still managed to speak of war in such terms after four years of being nearly entombed in the mud and carnage of Flanders. One Englishman writes of the "undoubted glamour" of the Western Front and adds "in the army or out of it, the wine of life is white and still, but at the Front it runs red and sparkling."[173] Or, "One crowded hour of glorious life/Is worth an age without a name."[174] The mortality of those who ventured forth on trench raids was high, but a Highlander writes without remorse that "I stepped forward and was chosen, along with fifty-two other chaps who were anxious to experience the zenith of trench excitement."[175] Nine out of the fifty-two returned.

If the modern reader is at all familiar with the true story of the General Staff's mismanagement that led to the slaughter of the British troops on the Somme, he is benumbed by this description of the battle as a pastoral idyll:

> Heavens! What a picture it was. What a grand picture of courage and discipline . . . . On they went over the field of vivid scarlet poppies, whose colours seemed to stand as a symbol of the fine red blood that was being shed so lavishly for the salvation of the world, while the sky-blue cornflowers, and the gleaming white of the chalk-lined trenches, together with the red poppies, gave the red, white and blue, the national colours of the British and French . . . .[176]

For an Aussie the romance is on a more personal level. "I rejoice though that I was a Scout and would not exchange my experiences with any, not even from the pages of *Boy's Own Paper*. Romance bathes the very name . . . ."[177] Another soldier of the Empire tells of the "evening amusement" of the C.E.F.; they "sneak up on the Germans, drop the grenades into the trenches, then hop in and beat hell out of the whole bunch, and then beat it back to their own trench."[178]

While the British still wrote of the excitement and glamor of war, it was the Americans who were most thrilled by the romantic call of the "Great Adventure." A rather vernacular captain in the Medical Corps proclaimed " 'It aint any of this 1898 Cuby War—but it's a nice war.' "[179] On their way to the "nice war," Doughboys are shown as dividing their time between retching over the rail and amusing themselves like a group of excited schoolboys going to a class picnic. "And the stories! Wow! And songs! Every song that was ever written did we sing . . . ."[180] One American narrator shows how this type of bubbling enthusiasm led him to enlist in the B.E.F. while the United States was still "neutral in thought and deed." "I had the fondness for adventure usual in young men. I liked to see the wheels go round. And so it happened that, when the war was about a year and a half old, I decided to get in before it was too late."[181] The story of the walrus-mustachioed recruiting sergeant's first reaction to the lad from the "colonies" must have made amusing reading for Americans who were now at war: " 'We ain't tykin no nootrals,' he said, with a sneer. And then: 'Better go back to Hamerika and 'elp Wilson write 'is blinkin notes.' "[182]

Upon reaching France, however, the ex-"nootral" entered enthusiastically into the excitement of trench warfare. Not only does he record for his readers how exciting his adventures were, but also boosts Yankee sportsmanship and ingenuity, for

> turning the corner of the next traverse, I saw Jerry drop his rifle and unlimber his persuader on a huge German who had just rounded the corner of the bay. He made a good job of it, getting him in the face, and must have simply caved him in, but not before he had thrown a bomb . . . .

> When I saw that bomb coming, I bunted at it like Ty Cobb trying to sacrifice. . . . I choked my bat and poked at the bomb instinctively, and by sheer good luck fouled the thing over the parapet.[183]

A young American found romance and excitement in merely driving a five-ton Pierce-Arrow truck. "As a result, I am becoming more as ye ancient adventurer who rode the moonlit highways long ago with a rapier by his side and a swear-word for a Bible."[184] Truck driving must have had its romantic appeal, for an American volunteer camion driver maintains "war's great caldron of heroism, praise, glory, poetry, music, brains, energy, flashes and grows, rustles and roars, fills the heavens with its mighty being . . . ."[185] In a moment of romantic ecstasy, he adds, "Oh! War as nothing else brings you back to the adventurous times of old."[186]

Nevil Monroe Hopkins, an American author of mystery stories, cannot see the death for the excitement, because

> I thrilled, and my heart pounded, as through a mist in that faint gray dawn I saw the German line advance! Again our bugle called—and then—I saw the gun near which I lay— the thrilling sight and sound will ever drill with me, it slid swiftly, silently, three feet back upon its mount—elastic and free.[187]

An American surgeon who refused to be disillusioned by seeing many horribly wounded men found excitement in dining at Verdun as part of his innocent adventure.

> We had hors d'oeuvres, consisting of sardines and sliced onion with bread and butter, omelette, beef with sauce tartare, potato salad, oranges and cakes. Jokes flew about, but they were harmless jokes. Neither then nor at any other time did I hear from French soldiers the coarse obscenity which too often mars the fighting man of other nations.[188]

Verdun was the scene of some of the bloodiest fighting of the century, but facts like this did not dim American enthusiasm when now I am right at the front, and with a commission, on the very day my country declares war. It seems as though my greatest and most impossible earthly longing has been granted. I am going to try to be worthy of it, and when I am facing anything hard in the future, I will remember I am an American soldier.[189]

A captain in the A.E.F. tells a narrator

"Do you know, man knows no keener joy in the world than that which I have to-night. Here I am in France at the head of two hundred and fifty men and horses and the guns and we're rolling up front to kick a dent in history. The poor unfortunate that ain't in this fight has almost got license to shoot himself. Life knows no keener joy than this."[190]

For the narrators who were portraying combat exploits in terms of nineteenth-century Romanticism, it was a " 'great time to be alive . . . . This place [France] is saturated with romance.' "[191]

It could all be so sylvan and lovely at times—"Luneville, a dream of fair women of old and new times [had] linden scents, and circling Taubes and little white puffs of shrapnel against blue skies."[192] Although they knew that they would experience the inevitable combat, many still thought in terms of the trappings and amenities of the great military adventure, for "in a sense it is a big adventure for them, and for some it will be 'the big adventure'—to come over the sea, all dressed up in new uniforms, to walk about the streets of Paris, before going on 'out there.' "[193]

Even after they moved eastward from Paris to the place names like Vaux, Soissons, Saint-Mihiel, and Meuse-Argonne that would forever be part of their lives and conversations, many would remain enthusiastic about the killing and death. After an American had bayoneted a German during a trench raid, he wrote of "the exhilaration of my exploit."[194] For the adventure-seeking Floyd Gibbons, "It was a beautiful sight, these men of ours going across those flat fields toward the tree clusters beyond from which the Germans poured a murderous machine gun fire."[195] A writer with literary inclinations emotes

> were I to tell you of the first thundering crash of a shell, the faint smell of battle and the distant incense of a gigantic spirit of the "Marseillaise" fighting for Victory . . . . I would be writing in one letter the wonders of the "Divine Comedy," of Boccaccio's "Sonnets," of Verlaine and Gibson and the unspelled poetry of Paradise itself.[196]

If one were wounded in writing verses for "the unspelled poetry of Paradise," he might come into contact with the American surgeon whose enthusiasm and naïvéte prompted him to write that "today for the first time since being over here we had a real surgical morning. Several distinguished visitors were present and the Major did four bully operations —alternating between two tables."[197]

With slang words like "bully" the inheritors of the spirit of Teddy Roosevelt came to France to seek adventure and glory, and the narrators of 1918 praised the "spirit of adventure . . . that brings us across the seas to the scene of danger."[198] A correspondent for the New York *Tribune* reacts like a schoolboy reading his first Tom Swift novel: "Verdun and Joffre, and 'they shall not pass,' and Napoleon's tomb, and war bread, and all the men with medals and everything. Great stuff! There'll never be anything like it in the world again. I tell you it's better than 'Ivanhoe.' Everything's happening and I'm in it."[199] The same writer relates the story of the United States general officer who in his excitement wanted to join the assault on his first visit to the Front. He pleaded, "I've just got to try and see if I can't bomb a few squareheads."[200] It is, however, an enlisted men's shipboard song that epitomizes the naïve, adventuresome spirit that

the narrators believed was ingrained in the Americans who
set forth on their "Great Adventure."

> Goodbye, pa; goodbye, ma:
> Goodbye mule, with your old hee-haw:
> I may not know what war's about,
> But I bet, by gosh, I'll soon find out.
> Goodbye, sweetheart, don't you care;
> I'll bring you a piece of the Kaiser's ear.
> I'll bring you a Turk and a German, too,
> And that's about all one fellow can do.[201]

It was a time for pride and glory; the reaction would come
later:

> I have seen the Glory of the Coming. I have watched the
> American Expeditionary Force grow from a small thing into
> a mighty thing—the mightiest thing, I veritably believe, that
> since conscious time began, has been undertaken by a free
> people with nothing personally to gain except honour, with
> nothing to keep except self-respect . . . our only territorial
> enlargement will be the graves where our fallen dead sleep
> on alien soil . . . we, as a world-power and as perhaps the
> most conspicuous example in our world, of a democracy, did
> our duty by ourselves, by our children, and their children
> and their children's children.[202]

When considered as a body, the narratives of 1918 show
the development of basically the same themes that comprised the 1914–1918 narratives. The romantic themes of
the "cause," religion, sacrifice, spiritual uplift, personal
manliness and courage, German degeneracy, Allied chivalry
and the thirst for excitement, glamour and adventure are all
present. What is different from 1917, however, is that the
body of the narratives were written by actual combatants,
for by 1918 soldiers with a literary bent could, usually upon
being wounded and sent home, find time to record their

impressions and experiences. Too, there is another difference that separates the 1918 narratives from the earlier ones, and a most important difference from the viewpoint of American studies; for the first time there were published a sizeable body of works written by Americans who actually served with American forces. It is, therefore, most interesting to note that the Doughboys' attitudes do not differ from the essentially romantic orientation of their Allied comrades of the four previous years.

Conclusion

Tales of the Great Adventure still cut through the sweet haze within American Legion halls across America. One tends to smile condescendingly at the veterans, and to relegate them and their tales to some dim filing-cabinet of history, along with plus-four knickers and expressions like "well, snap my gaiters!" Does the sophisticated modern student, however, really comprehend the social, intellectual and moral background that guided the Doughboys on their journey Over There, and thus understand the American mind of the period?

The study of the narratives has meaning and value if they are considered as evidence of the romantic orientation of the 1914–1918 American reading public, rather than as poorly written, soppy gasconades. Although a great number of them were obvious attempts at pro-Allied propaganda, and should be used with caution as source documents on such as German atrocities in Belgium, they still are illustrative social statements. While nearly all the writers took the same positive tone and approach to the war, one naturally wonders what happened to the anomalous disillusioned narrator who wrote during the war years. The best example concerns Ellen N. LaMotte, an American volunteer nurse in France who wrote a narrative of her hospital experiences and maintained that both the heroic and "backwash" stories of war are true. She writes "war, superb as it is, is not necessarily a filtering process by which men and nations may be purified."[1]

Whereas other narrators write of the sense of sacrifice and inspiration of the soldiers, she inveighs against war with somewhere, higher up, a handful of men had been able to impose upon Alphonse, and Hippolyte . . . and thousands like them, a state of mind which was not in them, of themselves. Base metal, gilded. And they were all harnessed to a great car, a Juggernaut, ponderous and crushing, upon which was enthroned Mammon, or Goddess of Liberty, or Reason, as you like.[2]

Some of her personal observations are devastating; for example, "Bah! The *Croix de Guerre* pinned to a night shirt, egg-stained and smelling of sweat!"[3] Her comment on the motivation of soldiers is equally as brutal and opposed to the mainstream of romantic thought of the period: "I was mobilized against my inclination. Now I have won the *Médalle Militaire*. My Captain won it for me. He made me brave. He had a revolver in his hand."[4] It is a strong reflection on the temper of the times that this narrative was not allowed to be sold in either France or the United Kingdom, or, after the spring of 1917, in America. Too, it is interesting to note that the volume was reprinted in 1934 during the depths of postwar cynicism.

The emotional composition of wartime America is strongly reflected in both the formal and informal machinery that existed in order to control opinions such as Miss LaMotte's. On June 16, 1917, President Wilson signed into law a weakened Espionage Act, which was limited when such men as Senators Lodge and Borah were successful in removing its press censorship provisions. Although Section III of the final act was elastic enough to allow for sedition prosecution, Congress went further, and on May 22, 1918, passed the Sedition Act. This legislation gave the Post Office Department and the Attorney General effective censorship powers, which, when combined with the Committee on Public Information (headed by a staunch New Freedom party worker, Colorado journalist George Creel), effectively monitored the communications media. It was, however, indirect pressure that caused the publisher to withdraw Ellen LaMotte's book from print. Such action appears to have been not uncommon, for the New York *Times* of May 18, 1918, reports that G. P. Putnam's Sons withdrew from sale at the informal request of the National Security League, the pacifistic Ellen Key's *War, Peace and the Future* published in 1917. Considering that patriotic emotions were so high that J. W. Ryndus of Athens, Illinois, accused of uttering pro-German sentiments, had an American flag tied around his neck and was forced to lead a Liberty Loan parade (New York *Times*, April 5, 1918), one must conclude that Ellen LaMotte's publishers were interested in their own survival.

It is also true that many intellectually aware Americans did not subscribe to the sentimental view of war presented by the narratives. An American studies scholar and participant in the war reacted to the bibliography of war narratives by saying that he had never heard of most of them and if he had

> I should have recognized—as I am sure others did—that much was propagandistic, that the "noble" books came from a type of writer, not from *all* writers, and that, even if the voices of maturity and balance were hushed, they were not totally absent. When our college president rose in April, 1917, and said to some 800 young men in chapel, "Thank God, war is declared," he was met with total silence.[5]

Too "not all Americans believed the stuff they read—and that, even if they did, it was from lack of true information and experience, and ignorance more than callousness toward suffering."[6]

Regardless, however, of how well-educated and sensitive Americans reacted to the emotional gushing that characterized the war books, many Americans revealed their visceral enthusiasm for the war by buying the books in large numbers even before the United States entered the war. As Mildred Aldrich perceptively noted in her introduction to a narrative, "These are the personal experiences which will be by no means its least interesting contribution to the students of the future who are to look back and try to understand this 'great adventure,' the most tragic and, we hope, the most glorious that humanity had yet encountered."[7] This understanding of the American mind of the war years is needed, for most students remember merely that World War I severely jolted the young writers and artists of America and led to the aesthetic and social rebellion of the Twenties. What many students do not fully understand is the dogmatically set values against which the young rebels were in protest. The birfurcation between the pre- and postwar generations became an unbridgeable gulf, or, as a modern literary critic writes, "The war is a definite dividing line between literary generations."[8] The older writers of the period sensed the coming alienation of their younger contemporaries; Edwin Arlington Robinson wrote of Thomas Sergeant Perry of Boston that " 'he knew, like many others, that the Great War had carried away with it the world that he had known, and in which he had best belonged.' "[9]

Shortly before World War II when there was much introspective reappraisal of the 1914–1918 encounter, Robert Nichols, the English editor of an anthology of Great War poetry, asked himself the whys of the disillusionment of the Twenties. He decided that "this is due to the presence in the individual of the notion of moral relativity. The cultivation of this notion—on the highly moral grounds of the necessity of a 'debunking' crusade—enables the individual to dodge a variety of extremely inconvenient ethical imperatives."[10] Such imperatives would include whether to struggle against an invasion attempt at Paris (or against the ovens at Dachau), or to reject the military experience and dodge responsibility (as did Yossarian in *Catch-22*). It is far easier to be cleverly cynical years after a war than to gain a perspective during a war, and John Dos Passos seems to understand this when he writes without bitterness of the young Americans fighting Hitler in a later war.

> For one thing I think the brutalities of war and oppression came as less of a shock to people who grew up in the thirties than they did to Americans of my generation, raised as we were during the quiet afterglow of the nineteenth century . . . .
> The boys who are fighting these present wars got their first ideas of the world during the depression years. From the time they first read the newspapers they drank in the brutalities of European politics with their breakfast coffee.[11]

It was this earlier generation which existed in the "afterglow" of the nineteenth century that authored the narratives that were the last gasp of an earlier and more romantic era. In fact, "An additional fracture between these two American literary generations . . . was certainly the extraordinary willingness of the older writers to lend their prestige and talent to the most bloodthirsty and archaic aspects of the war."[12] The reading public of 1914–1918 was largely unconscious of any impending "fracture" and accepted with approval the romanticism of the narratives. Clark S. Northup of Cornell University wrote in a 1917 journal an essay which expressed his enthusiasm for war literature. "Instead of songs of hatred," he said, "we are now reading narratives of personal experience, visions in the trenches, . . . admiration for deeds of courage and heroism."[13]

Indeed, the reading public had such admiration for the romantic narratives that H. H. Reckman in the *South Atlantic Quarterly* of July, 1918, complains that the bookshops were crammed with such "pot-boilers" as Sergeant

Empey's, Private Peat's and Arnold Bennett's,[14] and another contemporary reviewer adds that war books can be "literally measured in yards of book-shelf."[15] It helps one to understand the extent of the outpouring of war narratives when one learns that the editorial board for *True Stories of the Great War* (1918) considered over 8,000 stories and finally settled on a six-volume edition.

In considering these narratives as a mirror of the American mind, it is interesting to note that the American soldiers themselves often made enthusiastic comments about the narratives. An A.E.F. draftee told a narrator " 'but if you are going to write up these camps, tell them to send us more war books, books full of the real stuff; we eat 'em up!' "[16] Too, Julia C. Stimson notes that Conningsby Dawson's *Carry On* and Donald Hankey's *A Student in Arms* were extremely popular in the soldiers' hospitals in France.

In determining why these narratives were so popular, one is led to consider the attraction of romantic war literature in general. The historian David Levin quotes Francis Parkman as saying, " 'One reads of a battle,' he said, 'with the same kind of interest with which he beholds the grand destructive phenomena of nature—although one's feeling is far more intense here because the forces are living tides of human wrath and valor.' "[17] Considering romantic literature in this context, a literary critic of the postwar years notes "war feeds on the romantic spirit."[18] Moreover, this viewpoint is developed by a narrator of the Great War who was endowed with the all too rare gift of insight into his own times:

> We men are never content! In the dull routine of normal life we sigh for Romance, and sometimes seek to create it artificially, stimulating spurious passions, plunging into muddy depths in search of it. Now we have got it and we sigh for a quiet life. But some day those who have not died will say:

> "Thank God I have lived! I have loved, and endured, and trembled, and trembling, dared. I have had my Romance."[19]

The old-school American novelist Winston Churchill underlines the theory that the narratives merely reflect the period's romantic proclivities when he writes that "failure to realize that the American is at heart an idealist is to lack understanding of our national character."[20]

The result was that "thrills and escapes were more real to those at home and were listened to with more avidity than accounts of suffering and fatality."[21] The reader who felt the seductive appeal of romanticism could even read of the horrors of combat without having his idealism eroded; as Hamilton Mabie wrote in 1915, " 'To escape the sorrow, the pain, and renovating power of a great human experience, would be to miss one of the greatest lessons ever set for men to learn.' "[22]

One must conclude that the tone of the more than four-hundred narratives is romantic; bitter narratives such as Ellen LaMotte's *The Backwash of War* were exceptions. But this does not explain the tenets of the wartime romanticism, and how they dovetail with the framework of nineteenth-century American literary romanticism. The recurring themes of a "cause," sacrifice, individual worth and prowess, good struggling against evil, nature, individual renaissance and national progress, chivalry and excitement have been examined in detail as they are manifested in the 1917–1918 narratives. In discussing these war books, a postwar critic notes essentially these same themes because

> in them we find what from our national character we might expect—a consciousness of the evils of this greatest evil done by mankind, but a consciousness dimmed by sentimental regard for some vague ideal imagined in a non-existent beyond; a racial adaptability to appalling conditions; a sometimes humorous, sometimes disgusted tolerance of them; in a word, the romantic mind.[23]

A literary historian recently compiled a definition of American literary romanticism,[24] and it is most interesting to note that the narratives illustrate each of his points. The romantic characteristics of "vitality and a springtime freshness" are both reflected in the narrators' adoration of the Adamic Doughboy. "Patriotism" is an overriding theme of the narratives, and the "craving for infinite growth and development" is reflected in the narrators' contention that both soldiers and nations would be spiritually and morally developed via the war. The expansive idealism is seen in the "cause" itself, and the potentiality of the individual is emphasized by the narrators who saw the war as bringing to the surface the latent strength and beauty of the men. Central to romanticism is the concept of all reality sharing an organic unity; to the narrators, therefore, the Allies, Nature and God were one, while the Germans were on the outside and bent on destroying the unity. "Further, the romantics believed that the modern mind itself was in danger, from incomplete and perverted values, from a disproportionate emphasis upon some aspects of reality to the exclusion of others."[25] This is in keeping with the narrators' contention that the world had been suffering from an excess of selfish materialism and debilitating pacifism, and that the war was needed to restore the proper balance between ideals and reality. Indeed, "Instead of seeing the war as the doom of their culture, they believed it would bring about its revival: the war was a severe but necessary lesson in moral idealism."[26]

In his anthology of Great War poetry, *Heroes' Twilight*, Bernard Bergonzi makes the oft-repeated statement that the poets began the war believing in an anachronistic romanticism, but soon found that these beliefs were specious. Disillusionment set in and it still persists today, for Granville Hicks cautions that we should not react to the fiftieth anniversary of the war with "the tinsel of factitious glory."[27]

This bitterness is easily understood, for only those totally lacking in human sensitivity could deny that the war was an appalling bloodbath; the British casualties for the month of July, 1916, exceeded the entire Allied casualties for the battle of Waterloo, and it is estimated that at Verdun over 150,000 of the dead were never buried, but were simply allowed to putrefy into the soil. As one critic explained the poets' disillusionment:

> What men and women were experiencing and feeling after the holocaust of the Somme if not before, could no longer be given poetic expression by writers whose sensibilities had been conditioned in Edwardian days or earlier, and whose poetic conventions were worn-out even before the war started.[28]

During the war itself, however, the prevailing attitude was largely wrought from the substance of the romantic nineteenth century rather than from the realistic twentieth, and the personal war narratives published in America from 1914–1918 provide an interesting and extensive portrayal of the American mind of the period. These romantic beliefs which belonged to a period innocent of Maxim machine guns and Chauchat automatic rifles stayed imbedded in the fabric of the American mind until the blood-bath of the Great Adventure washed them out, and the young writers of the Twenties concentrated on their final destruction. For many of the common, aesthetically unsophisticated survivors, however, the romance of the war continues to provide a reality of nostalgia; in American Legion halls can still be heard a last verse to "Mademoiselle from Armentières":

> 'Twas a hell of a war as I recall,
> But a damned sight better than no war at all . . .

Notes

INTRODUCTION

1. David Levin, *History as Romantic Art* (Stanford, 1959), p. 11.
2. Henry F. May, *The End of American Innocence, 1912–1917* (New York, 1959), p. ix.
3. Laurence Stallings, *The Doughboys* (New York, 1963), p. 367. For an excellent short history of the war, see, Cyril B. Falls, *The Great War* (New York and London, 1960). Some of the best volumes on America's part in the war are: Ernest R. May, *The World War and American Isolation, 1914–1917* (Cambridge, Mass., 1959); Daniel M. Smith, *The Great Departure: The United States and World War I, 1914–1920* (New York, 1965); Frank Freidel, *Over There: The Story of America's First Great Overseas Crusade* (Boston, 1964).
4. Harold Peat, *Private Peat* (Indianapolis, 1917), p. 168.
5. Richard Watt, *Dare Call It Treason* (New York, 1963), p. 61.
6. F. Scott Fitzgerald, *Tender is the Night* (New York, 1933), pp. 56–57.
7. Personal letter to the author from Wilson Ober Clough, January 15, 1965. Professor Clough is referring to the war novels of the 1920's.
8. Personal letter to the author from Wilson Ober Clough, March 19, 1965.
9. Richard Chase, *The American Novel and Its Traditions* (New York, 1957), *passim.*
10. Donald Hankey, *A Student in Arms* (New York, 1917), p. 105.
11. Guy Empey, *Over the Top* (New York, 1917), p. 2.
12. Conningsby Dawson, *The Glory of the Trenches* (New York, 1918), p. 139.
13. Owen Wister, *The Pentecost of Calamity* (New York, 1915), p. 148.
14. Dawson, p. 12.
15. Wister, p. 115.
16. Dawson, p. 119.
17. May, p. 261.
18. Wister, p. 121.
19. Dorothy Canfield Fisher, *Home Fires in France* (New York, 1918), p. 75.
20. Dawson, p. 110.
21. Fisher, p. 171.

22. James R. McConnell, *Flying for France* (New York, 1917), p. 97.

23. Empey, p. 280.

24. Peat, p. 148.

25. Dawson, p. 131.

26. Peat, p. 147.

27. *Ibid.*, p. 201.

28. Dawson, p. 108.

29. Frederic Palmer, *My Year of the Great War* (New York, 1915), p. 464.

30. Wister, p. 86.

31. Francis Huard, *My Home in the Field of Honour* (New York, 1916), p. 259.

32. Mildred Aldrich, "The Little House on the Marne," *Atlantic Monthly*, CXVI (1915), 3.

33. Hankey, p. 84.

34. Dawson, p. 26.

35. *Ibid.*, p. 23.

36. Fisher, p. 71.

37. Dawson, p. 61.

38. Peat, p. 149.

39. Dawson, p. 116.

40. Empey, p. 233.

41. Dawson, p. 61.

42. Wister, p. 116.

43. Dawson, p. 14.

44. Arnold Bennett, *Over There* (New York, 1915), p. 60.

45. Aldrich, p. 7.

46. Levin, p. 7.

47. See the unpublished dissertations: Gerald E. Critoph, "The American Literary Reaction to World War I" (University of Pennsylvania, 1957); and James R. Conner, "Pen and Sword: World War I Novels in America, 1916–1941" (University of Wisconsin, 1961).

1917

1. E. Alexander Powell, *Italy at War* (New York, 1917), p. 139.

2. Frederic Palmer, *My Second Year of the War* (New York, 1917), p. 330.

3. Harry E. Brittain, *From Verdun to the Somme: An Anglo-American Glimpse of the Great Advance* (New York, 1917), p. ix.

4. Ernesta Drinker Bullitt, *An Uncensored Diary from the Central Empires* (New York, 1917), p. 160.

5. Brittain, p. 34.

6. Arthur H. Gleason, *Our Part in the Great War* (New York, 1917), p. 29.

7. *Ibid.*, p. 33.

8. *Ibid.*, p. 6.

9. *Ibid.*

10. Conningsby Dawson, *Carry On: Letters in War-Time* (New York, 1917), p. 131. Hereafter referred to as *Carry On*.

11. Mrs. Humphry Ward, *England's Effort* (New York, 1917), p. ix. Hereafter referred to as *England's Effort*.

12. Powell, p. 119.

13. Harry Butters, *Harry Butters, R.F.A.—"An American Citizen"* (New York, 1917), p. 242.

14. Lord Northcliffe, *Lord Northcliffe's War Book* (New York, 1917), p. 43.

15. As quoted in Henry Van Dyke, *Fighting for Peace* (New York, 1917), pp. 158–159.

16. *Ibid.*, p. 7.

17. Winston Churchill, *A Traveller in War-Time* (New York, 1917), p. 108.

18. Carita Spencer, *War Scenes I Shall Never Forget* (New York, 1917), p. 9.

19. Van Dyke, p. 155.

20. Mrs. Humphry Ward, *Towards the Goal* (New York, 1917), p. viii. Hereafter referred to as *Towards the Goal*.

21. See the unpublished dissertation by Gerald E. Critoph, "The American Literary Reaction to World War I" (University of Pennsylvania, 1957), p. 142.

22. *Ibid.*, p. 162 and *passim*.

23. George Clark Musgrave, *Under Four Flags for France* (New York, 1918), p. 342. Although this was published in early 1918, it was written in 1917 before America had entered the war.

24. *Ibid.*, p. 339.

25. Ian Hay [John Beith], *The First Hundred Thousand* (New York, 1917), p. 182. Hereafter referred to as *Hundred Thousand*.

26. Brittain, p. 12.

27. *Carry-On*, p. 25.

28. Butters, pp. 173–174.

29. *England's Effort*, p. 164.

30. *Ibid.*, p. 208.

31. Brittain, p. xv.

32. Harold Peat, *Private Peat* (Indianapolis, 1917), p. 86.

33. Butters, p. 173.

34. Louis Keene, *"Crumps": The Plain Story of a Canadian Who Went* (Boston, 1917), p. 31.

35. Alan Seeger, *Letters and Diary* (New York, 1917), p. 126.

36. *Carry-On*, p. 86.

37. Anon., *Wounded and a Prisoner of War* (New York, 1917), p. 157. Hereafter referred to as *Wounded*.

38. Gleason, pp. 150–151.

39. *Ibid.*, p. 87.

40. *Carry-On*, p. 127.

41. Butters, p. 24.

42. Victor Chapman, *Victor Chapman's Letters from France* (New York, 1917), p. 42.

43. Seeger, p. 126.

44. Norman Prince, *A Volunteer Who Died for the Cause He Loved* (Boston, 1917), p. 1.

45. Seeger, p. 109.

46. René Nicolas, *Campaign Diary of a French Officer* (Boston, 1917), p. 138.

47. A. J. Dawson, *For France* (New York, 1917), p. 160.

48. *Ibid.*, p. 161.

49. Peat, p. 162.

50. Seeger, p. 211.

51. Chapman, p. 31.

52. *Hundred Thousand*, p. 161.

53. *Wounded*, p. 159.

54. Butters, p. 226.

55. *Carry-On*, p. 45.

56. Nobbs, p. 146.

57. Peat, p. 85.

58. Pierre Loti [Julien Viaud], *War* (Philadelphia, 1917), p. 320.

59. Mildred Aldrich, *On the Edge of the War Zone* (Boston, 1917), p. 76.

60. A. J. Dawson, p. 2.

61. Ian Hay [John Beith] *All in It* (New York, 1917), p. 195. Hereafter referred to as *All in It*.

62. Aldrich, p. 27.

63. *Towards the Goal*, pp. 134–135.

64. Francis Wilson Huard, *My Home in the Field of Mercy* (New York, 1917), p. 71.

65. Gleason, p. 215.

66. Emmet Crozier, *American Reporters on the Western Front, 1914–1918* (New York, 1959), *passim*.

67. *Wounded*, p. 153.

68. Anon., *A German Deserter's War Experiences* (New York, 1917), p. 5.

69. Butters, p. 250.

70. Keene, p. 59.

71. Gleason, p. 16.

72. *Carry-On*, p. 35.

73. Seeger, p. 8.

74. *All in It*, p. 135.

75. *Carry-On*, p. 124.

76. *Ibid.*, p. 76.

77. Seeger, p. 66.

78. Arthur Guy Empey, *"Over the Top," by an American Soldier Who Went* (New York, 1917), p. 64.

79. *Ibid.*, p. 245.

80. Keene, p. 109.

81. Nicolas, p. 56.

82. Northcliffe, p. 48.

83. Powell, p. 213.

84. *All in It*, p. 210.

85. *Ibid.*, p. 123.

86. *Ibid.*, p. 44.

87. A. J. Dawson, p. 103.

88. James Norman Hall, *Kitchener's Mob: The Adventures of an American in the British Army* (New York, 1916), p. 145. Hereafter referred to as *Kitchener's Mob*.

89. Keene, p. 20.

90. *Wounded*, p. 112.

91. Nicolas, p. 71.

92. Loti, p. 70.

93. *Carry-On*, p. 17.

94. Nobbs, p. 43.

95. *Carry-On*, p. 8.

96. *Ibid.*, p. 43.

97. Butters, p. 231.

98. Conningsby Dawson, *The Glory of the Trenches* (New York, 1917), p. 86. Hereafter referred to as *Glory*.

99. *Carry-On*, p. 52.

100. Butters, p. 23.

101. *Carry-On*, pp. 14–15.

102. Butters, p. 192.

103. *Carry-On*, p. 5.

104. Nobbs, p. 86.

105. A. J. Dawson, p. 73.

106. *Ibid.*, p. 2.

107. *Wounded*, p. 218.

108. *Carry-On*, p. 18.

109. Chapman, p. 4.

110. *Ibid.*, p. 183.
111. *Ibid.*, p. 17.
112. James R. McConnell, *Flying for France* (New York, 1917), p. 131.
113. Chapman, p. 25.
114. *Ibid.*, p. 36.
115. Prince, p. 75.
116. James Norman Hall, *High Adventure* (New York, 1917), p. 184. Hereafter referred to as *High Adventure.*
117. Nobbs, p. 158.
118. *High Adventure*, p. 150.
119. *Kitchener's Mob*, p. 99.
120. *Ibid.*, p. 98.
121. Seeger, p. 205.
122. Butters, p. 123.
123. *Carry-On*, p. 60.
124. Seeger, p. 93.
125. *High Adventure*, p. 135.
126. *Kitchener's Mob*, p. 45.
127. Keene, p. 8.
128. Butters, p. 162.
129. Seeger, p. 154.
130. *Kitchener's Mob*, p. 2.
131. Keene, p. 66.
132. Gleason, p. 62.
133. *Ibid.*, p. 48.
134. *Ibid.*, p. 38.
135. *Kitchener's Mob*, p. 92.
136. Butters, p. 133.
137. Nicolas, p. 87.
138. Chapman, p. 158.
139. Seeger, p. 40.
140. Nicolas, pp. 60–61.

1918

1. Barrie Pitt, *1918: The Last Act* (New York, 1964), p. 2.
2. Esther Sayles Root and Marjorie Crocker, *Over Periscope Pond* (Boston, 1918), p. 212.
3. Fullerton L. Waldo, *America at the Front* (New York, 1918), p. 20.
4. Charles H. Grasty, *Flashes from the Front* (New York, 1918), p. 160.

5. *Ibid.*, p. 147.

6. Mrs. Frank Wilmot, *Oregon Boys in the War* (Portland, Oregon, 1918), p. 18.

7. Pitt, p. 63.

8. Wilmot, p. 18.

9. Wainwright Merrill, *A College Man in Khaki* (New York, 1918), p. 39.

10. See the unpublished dissertation by Gerald E. Critoph, "The American Literary Reaction to World War I" (University of Pennsylvania, 1957), p. 283.

11. An anonymous poem quoted in Isabel Anderson, *Zigzagging* (Boston, 1918), p. 159.

12. R. Douglas Pinkerton, *"Ladies from Hell"* (New York, 1918), p. 254.

13. Reginald Grant, *S.O.S. Stand To!* (New York, 1918), p. i.

14. R. Hugh Knyvett, *"Over There" with the Australians* (New York, 1918), p. i.

15. Pinkerton, p. 48.

16. Merrill, p. 213.

17. Joseph L. Smith, *Over There and Back in Three Uniforms* (New York, 1918), p. 19.

18. *Ibid.*, p. 153.

19. Albert N. Depew, *Gunner Depew* (Chicago, 1918), p. 23.

20. E. M. Roberts, *Flying Fighter* (New York, 1918), p. 91.

21. Smith, p. 22.

22. Jack Morris Wright, *A Poet of the Air* (Boston, 1918), p. 29.

23. Smith, p. 17.

24. Arthur Guy Empey, *First Call* (New York, 1918), p. 6. Hereafter referred to as *First Call*.

25. Briggs Kilburn Adams, *The American Spirit* (Boston, 1918), p. 43.

26. Bertram Bernheim, *Passed as Censored* (Philadelphia, 1918), p. 122.

27. Winston Churchill, *A Traveller in War-Time* (New York, 1918), p. 9.

28. Edwin Austin Abbey, *An American Soldier* (Boston, 1918), p. 3.

29. Knyvett, pp. 317–318.

30. R. Derby Holmes, *A Yankee in the Trenches* (Boston, 1918), p. 199.

31. *True Stories of the Great War* (New York, 1918), p. i.

32. Wright, p. 34.

33. Floyd Gibbons, *And They Thought We Wouldn't Fight* (New York, 1918), p. 8,

34. Wright, p. 41.

35. Smith, p. 49.

36. R. Douglas Pinkerton, *Ladies from Hell* (New York, 1918), p. 63.

37. Depew, p. 65.

38. Knyvett, p. 115.

39. William Redmond, *Trench Pictures from France* (New York, 1918), p. 63.

40. Preston Gibson, *Battering the Boche* (New York, 1918), p. 96.

41. Thomas Tiplady, *The Soul of the Soldier* (New York, 1918), p. 123.

42. *True Stories*, p. iv.

43. Root, p. 131.

44. Charles W. Whitehair, *Out There* (New York, 1918), p. 249.

45. *Ibid.*, p. 189.

46. Laurence Stallings, *The Doughboys* (New York, 1963), pp. 180–181.

47. Joseph H. Odell, *The New Spirit of the New Army* (New York, 1918), p. 28.

48. Tiplady, p. 10.

49. Smith, p. 53.

50. Glenn H. Vail, *Lest We Forget* (New York, n.d.), p. 7.

51. Abbey, p. 92.

52. Knyvett, p. 322.

53. Merrill, p. 111.

54. Adams, p. 79.

55. Wright, p. x.

56. *Ibid.*, p. 46.

57. Harry Lauder, *A Minstrel in France* (New York, 1918), p. 204.

58. Joseph H. Odell, *The New Spirit of the New Army* (New York, 1918), p. 28.

59. Mildred Aldrich, *The Peak of the Load* (Boston, 1918), p. 3.

60. Abbey, p. 77.

61. Tiplady, p. 208.

62. Whitehair, p. 119.

63. Julia C. Stimson, *Finding Themselves* (New York, 1918), p. 60.

64. Baron C. Buffin, *Brave Belgians*, trans. A. Halland (New York, 1918), p. 114.

65. Tiplady, p. 186.

66. Ian Hay [John Beith], *Getting Together* (New York, 1918), p. 13.

67. Tiplady, p. 162.

68. Pat O'Brien, *Outwitting the Hun* (New York, 1918), p. 5.

69. Knyvett, p. 325.

70. *Ibid.*, p. 326.

71. Henriette Curvu-Magot, *Beyond the Marne*, trans. Katherine Babbitt (Boston, 1918), p. 107.

72. Stimson, p. 161.

73. Whitehair, p. 97.

74. *Ibid.*, p. 96.

75. William L. Stidger, *Soldier Silhouettes on Our Front* (New York, 1918), p. 50.

76. Smith, pp. 50–51.

77. *Ibid.*, p. 179.

78. Abbey, p. 106.

79. Pinkerton, p. 83.

80. Wilmot, p. 139.

81. Gibbons, p. 220.

82. Adams, p. 53.

83. Abbey, p. 165.

84. Wright, pp. 142–143.

85. Gibbons, p. 298.

86. Redmond, p. 42.

87. Pinkerton, p. 105.

88. Anderson, p. 171.

89. Stidger, p. 45.

90. Gibbons, p. 338.

91. Irvin Shrewsbury Cobb, *The Glory of the Coming* (New York, 1918), pp. 461–462.

92. Stimson, p. 81.

93. Root, p. 186.

94. Knyvett, p. 174.

95. Depew, p. 70.

96. Grant, p. 172.

97. Knyvett, p. 315.

98. Grant, p. 232.

99. Pinkerton, p. 242.

100. Tiplady, p. 16.

101. *Ibid.*, pp. 230–231.

102. Dugmore, p. 45.

103. Pinkerton, p. 185.

104. David Fallon, *The Big Fight* (New York, 1918), p. 117.

105. Manfred Freiberr von Richthofen, *Red Battle Flyer* (New York, 1918), p. 47.

106. Pinkerton, p. 237.

107. Gibson, p. 59.

108. Pinkerton, p. 162.

109. Holmes, p. 144.
110. Buffin, p. 157.
111. Malcolm Cummings Grow, *Surgeon Grow* (New York, 1918), p. 252.
112. Depew, p. 159.
113. *Ibid.*, p. 70.
114. *Ibid.*, p. 76.
115. Grant, p. 212.
116. *Ibid.*, p. 96.
117. *Ibid.*, p. 99.
118. Pinkerton, p. 51.
119. *Ibid.*, p. 76.
120. Edward George Downing Liveing, *Attack* (New York, 1918), p. 47.
121. *Ibid.*, p. 75.
122. Holmes, p. 113.
123. Pinkerton, p. 81.
124. Tiplady, p. 129.
125. Arthur Guy Empey, *Tales from a Dugout* (New York, 1918), p. ii.
126. Knyvett, p. 112.
127. *Ibid.*, p. 318.
128. *Ibid.*, p. 234.
129. Gibson, p. 27.
130. Bernheim, p. 116.
131. Gibson, p. 105.
132. Gibbons, p. 228.
133. Waldo, p. 128.
134. *Ibid.*, p. 31.
135. Musgrave, pp. 367–368.
136. Waldo, p. 21.
137. Heywood Broun, *The A.E.F.* (New York, 1918), p. 17.
138. *Ibid.*, p. 262.
139. Adams, p. 8.
140. Wilmot, p. 33.
141. *Ibid.*, p. 36.
142. *Ibid.*, p. 35.
143. Gibbons, p. 217.
144. Bernheim, p. 29.
145. Gibbons, p. 193.
146. Bernheim, p. 39.
147. Gibbons, p. 373.
148. *Ibid.*, p. 304.
149. Wilmot, p. 114.

150. Tiplady, p. 24.
151. Gibson, p. 46.
152. Stimson, p. 88.
153. Edith O'Shaughnessy, *My Lorraine Journal* (New York, 1918), p. 46.
154. E. M. Roberts, *A Flying Fighter* (New York, 1918), pp. 52–53.
155. Wilmot, p. 80.
156. Grasty, p. 299.
157. O'Brien, p. 38.
158. Richthofen, p. 94.
159. Roberts, p. 150.
160. *Ibid.*, p. 160.
161. *True Stories*, p. iv.
162. Wright, p. 236.
163. *Ibid.*, p. 128.
164. Wilmot, p. 140.
165. Grant, p. 32.
166. Smith, p. 15.
167. Dugmore, p. 181.
168. Roberts, p. 255.
169. Smith, p. 91.
170. Roy A. Christian, *Roy's Trip to the Battlefields of Europe* (Chambersburg, Pennsylvania, 1918), p. 109.
171. *Ibid.*, p. 202.
172. Wright, p. 106.
173. Tiplady, p. 41.
174. *Ibid.*, p. 51.
175. Pinkerton, p. 101.
176. Dugmore, p. 198.
177. Knyvett, p. 3.
178. Bernheim, p. 32.
179. *Ibid.*, p. 17.
180. *Ibid.*, pp. 10–11.
181. Holmes, p. 2.
182. *Ibid.*, p. 8.
183. *Ibid.*, p. 35.
184. Wright, p. 14.
185. *Ibid.*, p. 26.
186. *Ibid.*, p. 19.
187. Nevil Monroe Hopkins, *Over the Threshold of War* (Philadelphia, 1918), p. 306.
188. William Townsend Porter, *Shock at the Front* (Boston, 1918), p. 113.
189. Abbey, p. 162.

190. Gibbons, p. 209.
191. *Ibid.*, p. 116.
192. O'Shaughnessy, p. 18.
193. Aldrich, p. 100.
194. Roberts, p. 88.
195. Gibbons, p. 296.
196. Wright, p. 12.
197. Bernheim, p. 26.
198. Grasty, p. 39.
199. Broun, p. 298.
200. *Ibid.*, p. 235.
201. Waldo, p. 1.
202. Cobb, p. x.

CONCLUSION

1. Ellen N. LaMotte, *The Backwash of War* (New York, 1916), p. 105.
2. *Ibid.*, p. 12.
3. *Ibid.*, p. 39.
4. *Ibid.*, p. 125.
5. Personal letter to the author from Wilson Ober Clough, April 26, 1967.
6. *Ibid.* Professor Clough kindly read the original draft of this book and offered valuable advice.
7. Thomasina Atkins, *The Letters of Thomasina Atkins* (New York, 1918), p. vii.
8. Charles A. Fenton, "A Literary Fracture of World War I," *American Quarterly*, XII (1960), 119.
9. *Ibid.*, p. 120.
10. Robert Nichols, editor, *Anthology of War Poetry* (London, 1943), p. 24.
11. John Dos Passos, *First Encounter*, revised edition (New York, 1945), p. 8.
12. Fenton, p. 119.
13. Clark S. Northup, "War and Literature," *Sewanee Review*, XXV (1917), 344.
14. H. H. Peckman, "War and Pot-Boilers," *South Atlantic Quarterly*, XVII (1918), 186.
15. Philip Tillinghast, "War Books," *The Bookman*, XLI (1915), 329.
16. Joseph H. Odell, *The New Spirit of the New Army* (New York, 1918), p. 41.

17. David Levin, *History as Romantic Art* (Stanford, 1959), p. 18.

18. W. H. Hindle, "War Books and Peace Propaganda," *The Bookman*, XXCI (1931), 159.

19. Donald Hankey, *A Student in Arms* (New York, 1917), p. 105.

20. Winston Churchill, *A Traveller in War-Time* (New York, 1918), p. 99.

21. Nichols, p. 60.

22. Fenton, p. 127.

23. Hindle, p. 159.

24. Richard Harter Fogle, *The Romantic Movement in American Writing* (New York, 1966), pp. 1–5.

25. *Ibid.*, p. 5.

26. Henry F. May, *The End of American Innocence, 1912–1917* (New York, 1959), p. 363.

27. Granville Hicks, "Hearts, Flowers and Machine Guns," *Saturday Review of Literature*, XLIX (January 15, 1966), 32.

28. I. M. Parsons, *Men Who March Away* (New York, 1965), p. 14.

An Annotated Bibliography of Personal War Narratives Published in America 1914-1918

A NOTE ON BIBLIOGRAPHY

This annotated bibliography is the only extensive listing of personal war narratives published in America, 1914–1918. There are probably some omissions both because some narratives were privately published and had limited circulation and because others simply escaped the trade lists.

The *United States Catalog*, 1914–1918, provided a bibliographical starting point, for the listings under "European War, Personal Narratives" were extensive, but not complete. The New York (City) Public Library's *Subject Catalog of the World War I Collection* (Boston: Hall, 1957) provided additional material, as did the following bibliographies:

Adams, E. D. *The Hoover War Collection at Stanford University, California.* Palo Alto: Stanford University Press, 1927.

Dawson, Loleta Irene. *European War Fiction in English.* Boston: Faxon, 1921.

Falls, Cyril. *War Books: A Critical Guide.* London: Davies, 1930.

Hart, Albert Bushnell. *America at War: A Handbook of Patriotic Education References.* New York: Doran, 1918.

Lang, Frederick W. T. *Books on the Great War.* London: Faber, 1916.

McKinley, Albert E. *Collected Materials for the Study of the War.* Philadelphia: McKinley, 1918.

Princeton University Library. *European War Collection.* Princeton: Princeton University Press, 1917.

Richardson, Ernest Cushing. *The Bibliography of the War.* Chicago: Bibliographical Society of America, 1919.

Smith, R. L. "Some Bibliographies of the European War and Its Causes," *Bulletin of Bibliography*, Vol. X, no. 3 (July-September, 1918), pp. 50–52.

The combined collections of the University of California (Berkeley and Los Angeles), the University of Southern California, the Los Angeles City and County Library and the California State Library (Sacramento) contain the bulk of the volumes listed in the bibliography. In cases where the narratives were not available, contemporary reviews in *Bookman, Dial, Literary Digest, New Republic,* New York *Times,* and *Review of Reviews* were studied in order to discover the nature of the subject matter; in relatively few instances, nothing was available on the book except the publication data.

Aaronsohn, Alexander. *With the Turks in Palestine.* Boston: Houghton Mifflin, 1916.

The story of an immigrant to America who, after having applied for United States citizenship, went abroad and was drafted into the Turkish army.

Abbey, Edwin Austin. *An American Soldier*. Boston: Houghton Mifflin, 1918.
This is a collection of letters from an American in the C.E.F. Little action is described, but there is much on the necessity of the cause and on the narrator's willingness to sacrifice himself; he was killed at Vimy Ridge in 1917.

Adams, Briggs Kilburn. *The American Spirit*. Boston: Atlantic Monthly Press, 1918.
Contains a foreword by Arthur Stanwood Pier, the narrator's English professor at Harvard, who writes: "All who love or serve Harvard University—and indeed all lovers of noble young men—must read these letters with a renewed sense of spiritual education." The narrator was killed while a pilot in the Royal Flying Corps.

Adams, G. *Behind the Scenes at the Front*. New York: Duffield, 1915.

Adams, John Bernard Pye. *Nothing of Importance: Eight Months at the Front with a Welsh Battalion*. New York, 1918.
A British captain, killed in action, balances the descriptions of the death and filth of war with comments on its glamour and excitement.

Aldrich, Mildred. *Hilltop on the Marne*. Boston: Small, Maynard, 1915.
An American ex-drama critic gives her impressions of the early months of the war, which she viewed from her cottage near the Marne River. This first appeared in the *Atlantic Monthly*, and became a best-seller in book form.

———. *On the Edge of the War Zone*. Boston: Small, Maynard, 1917.

A continuation of the above, this volume is decidedly pro-British in tone. Essentially romantic in orientation, the author is at least realistic enough to see the contradiction in singing "Peace on Earth" at Christmas while men are locked in combat.

――――. *The Peak of the Load.* Boston: Small, Maynard, 1918.
Epistolary in form, this is the final volume of the series. She is delighted by America's entry into the war, and gives romantic descriptions of the first American troops to arrive in France.

Alexander, H. M. *On Two Fronts.* New York: Dutton, 1917.

Allen, H. W. *Unbroken Line.* New York: Dutton, 1917.

American Ambulance Field Service: Diary of Section 8. Boston: Todd, 1917.
A privately printed record of America's "University Gentlemen" who volunteered as ambulance drivers.

Anderson, Isabel. *Zigzagging.* Boston: Houghton Mifflin, 1918.
Mrs. Anderson writes intelligently about her hospital and canteen work in France, although much of her experience was a guided tour.

Anonymous. *A German Deserter's War Experience,* trans. by J. Koettgen. New York: Huebsch, 1917.
This narrative was serialized in a New York socialist newspaper and the book went through three printings in America. Although mainly a militant socialist tract that includes stories of enlisted men shooting officers for the cause of the revolution, it also presents a devastating picture of the German army. Full propaganda value is realized through the use of atrocity stories and descriptions of the Prussian caste structure.

Anzac [pseud.]. *On the Anzac Trail.* Philadelphia: Lippincott, 1916.
An enthusiastic account of the campaign in Gallipoli; the
narrative reflects no bitterness, although the author was dis-
abled.

Ashe, E. H. *Intimate Letters from France during America's
First Year of War.* San Francisco: Philopolis Press, 1918.
These are a Red Cross worker's letters about suffering in
Belgium and France during 1917.

Askew, Alice J. *The Stricken Land: Serbia as We Saw It.*
New York: Dodd, Mead, 1916.
The author, attached to the First British Field Hospital for
Serbia, presents a record of civilian suffering.

Atkins, Thomasina [pseud.]. *The Letters of Thomasina Atkins.* New York: Doran, 1918.
This is the narrative of an ex-actress who tells of the rigors
of the Women's Auxiliary Army Corps.

Austin, W. *War Zone Gadabout.* Boston: W. Austin, 1917.

Austrian, D. *Ways of War and Peace.* New York: Stanhope,
Dodge, 1914.

Bairnsfather, Bruce. *Bullets and Billets.* New York: Putnam,
1916.
The famous London cartoonist, the creator of soldier characters Bill, Bert and Alf, describes with verve and excitement
his life at the Front.

Baldwin, Harold. *Holding the Line.* Chicago: McClurg, 1918.
The narrator, who lost a leg in action with the Canadians,
slants his volume toward the A.E.F., and attempts to inspire
the American soldiers.

Beaufort, J. M. de. *Behind the German Veil.* New York: Dodd, Mead, 1918.
The American narrator was a correspondent for the *London Telegraph* who, by describing life in Germany, tries to lift the propaganda veil which he assumes the Germans have used in the United States to hide their true character.

Bell, Frederick McKelvey. *First Canadians in France.* New York: Doran, 1917.
A colonel in the Medical Corps writes of the medical service and the wounded in a light, romantic manner.

Bell, Ralph W. *Canada in War-Paint.* New York: Dutton, 1917.
This is a collection of semi-humorous sketches of the C.E.F. on the Western Front.

Belmont, Ferdinand. *Crusader of France*, trans. G. F. Lees. New York: Dutton, 1917.
Letters from a sous-lieutenant, killed in 1915; he expressed an overpowering, religious faith in the cause.

Belton, James and Ernest Gregory Odell. *Hunting the Hun.* New York: Appleton, 1918.
Similar in style to the famous *Over the Top*, this narrative gives a plain, realistic account of life in the British trenches.

Benedict, C. *Six Months, March-August, 1914.* New York: C. Benedict, 1914.
Privately printed.

Bennett, Arnold. *Over There.* New York: Methuen, 1915.
A popular novelist and short-story author reports on his tour of the British and French fronts in 1915; contains some excellent Parisian sketches.

Benson, S. C. *Back from Hell.* Chicago: McClurg, 1918.

Bernheim, Bertram M. *Passed as Censored.* Philadelphia: Lippincott, 1917.
The author is an American businessman who goes off on the "Big Adventure," and becomes an officer in the Services of the Rear. He believes that America is in the "crusade for righteousness."

Beury, C. E. *Russia after the Revolution.* Philadelphia: Jacobs, 1918.

Beveridge, Albert Jeremiah. *What Is Back of the War.* Indianapolis: Bobbs-Merrill, 1915.
The Indiana senator attempts to present a "balanced" picture of the fighting by visiting both sides. Opposed to American intervention.

Bigelow, Glenna Lindsay. *Liege on the Line of the March.* New York: Lane, 1918.
An American girl who was caught as the Germans invaded Belgium and later released tells her story, with emphasis on the bravery of the Belgians.

Bishop, William A. *Winged Warfare.* New York: Doran, 1918.
An "ace" flyer of the Royal Flying Corps tells of his forty-seven German kills, and emphasizes the excitement and chivalry of the air war.

Bolwell, F. A. *With a Reservist in France.* New York: Dutton, 1917.

Bourcier Emmanuel. *Under the German Shells*, trans. G. N. and M. R. Holt. New York: Scribner's, 1918.
This records the experiences of a French officer who was later on duty in America instructing the A.E.F. He records the mass death, but mainly eulogizes the spirit of the *poilu.*

Bowe, J. *Soldiers of the Legion.* New York: MacGregor, 1918.

Boyd, William. *With a Field Ambulance at Ypres, being letters written March 7–August 15, 1915.* New York: Doran, 1916.
A record of courage and suffering with the B.E.F. in Flanders; this life has a peculiar fascination of its own.

Bradley, Amy Owen. *Back of the Front in France.* Boston: Butterfield, 1918.
This narrative consists of the letters of an American girl who was a volunteer charity worker in France; she was most impressed by the sacrificial nature of French suffering.

Brittain, Harry E. *From Verdun to the Somme: An Anglo-American Glimpse of the Great Advance.* New York: Lane, 1917.
The author, who traveled to France with Representative James Beck, is extremely romantic toward the cause to the point of applying the Gettysburg Address to the Great War. He is proud of the American volunteers in France, and sheds many tears over the Rheims Cathedral's destruction.

Broun, Heywood. *The A.E.F.* New York: Appleton, 1918.
This volume is really a collection of the reporter's columns that were published in the *New York Tribune*; good record of the nadir of the American forces.

Bryan, Julien Hequembough. *Ambulance 464.* New York: Macmillan, 1918.
The author was a seventeen-year-old volunteer ambulance driver, who left Princeton for France. He admits that he went over for excitement, but that he quickly became imbued with the French spirit.

Buffin, Baron C. *Brave Belgians,* trans. A. Hallard. New York: Putnam, 1918.

An anthology of romantic stories concerning the exploits of Belgian soldiers.

Bullitt, Ernesta Drinker. *An Uncensored Diary from the Central Empire.* New York: Doubleday, 1917.
A United States tourist describes a grim, hateful and impoverished Germany; she dislikes German efficiency, but respects it, and is only mildly anti-German. This was written while America was still "neutral."

Bundle of Letters from Belgian Friends. Bristol, Rhode Island: North, 1916.
Privately printed.

Burgess, Gelett. *War—the Creator.* New York: Huebsch, 1916.
First appearing in *Collier's*, this is a romanticized narrative of how combat helps a French youth find manhood.

Burke, Kathleen. *White Road to Verdun.* New York: Doran, 1916.
A record of hospital work and of the courage of France, this narrative was written by a Scottish volunteer worker who went on a fund-raising tour of America.

Burry, Herbert. *Here and There in the War Area.* Milwaukee: Young, 1916.
Bishop Burry pictures the war as a fount for Christian revival; published by the Episcopal Church.

Buswell, Leslie. *Ambulance No. 10: Personal Letters from the Front.* New York: Houghton Mifflin, 1915.
This volume, which carries a recruiting poster at the end, stressed the excitement and chivalry involved in the work of the college volunteers in France. The editor himself won the Croix de Guerre.

Butters, Harry. *Harry Butters, R.F.A.*—"An American Citizen." New York: Lane, 1918.
This is comprised of the letters of a wealthy young Californian who volunteered for the British forces and was killed in France. Although his letters show that he wants America to enter the war, they do not reflect a hatred of Germans as much as they show a thirst for excitement.

Cable, Boyd. *Between the Lines.* New York: Dutton, 1915.
The author proposes to give the background behind the brief press releases on the war; as a reporter, he is quite realistic, but does emphasize the cheerfulness of Tommy Atkins.

————. *Grapes of Wrath.* New York: Dutton, 1917.
Centered on the Somme, this volume reflects the author's attempt to show that the soldiers' dedication during the Great War was unsurpassed even by the soldiers of Julia Ward Howe's time.

Cameron, John Stanley. *Ten Months in a German Raider: A Prisoner of War Aboard the Wolf.* New York: Doran, 1918.
An American merchant captain tries to show the Germans as barbarians, but his narrative shows that he really received quite adequate treatment.

Camion Letters from American College Men. New York: Holt, 1918.
This epistolary narrative reflects the youthful enthusiasm and dash of American collegians in France.

Camp, Charles Wadsworth. *War's Dark Frame.* New York: Dodd, 1917.
An English war correspondent presents a picture of trench life that is realistic but not bitter.

Campbell, G. *Soldier of the Sky.* Chicago: Davis, 1918.

————. *Verdun to the Vosges: Impressions of the War on the Fortress Frontier of Europe.* New York: Longmans, 1916.
A *London Times* correspondent presents a vivid description of the early days of the war, and stresses the extent of French heroism.

Canfield, Dorothy. *Home Fires in France.* New York: Holt, 1918.
The American writer relates her experiences in France as a civilian observer, and her romantic treatment of the French leaves no doubt as to her lack of "neutrality."

Capart, G. P. *Blue Devil of France.* New York: Watt, 1918.

Casalis, Alfred Eugene: *For France and the Faith,* trans. by W. E. Bristol. New York: Association Press, 1917.
This narrative consists of letters of a French theological student who enlisted, and is designed to provide spiritual inspiration for soldiers.

Cassels, Joe. *Black Watch: A Record in Action.* New York: Doubleday, 1918.
A British professional soldier who went to France in 1914 dwells on the gallantry and *esprit de corps* of the Highland regiment.

Castle, Agnes and Egerton. *Little House in War Time.* New York: Dutton, 1916.
A woman of gentility views the war lightly from an English country home.

Casualty (pseud.). *"Contemptible."* Philadelphia: Lippincott, 1916.
This is the diary of a British regular officer who served in 1914; interested primarily in tactics.

Chapin, Harold. *Soldier and Dramatist.* New York: Lane, 1916.

These are the letters of an American playwright who lived in England, volunteered, and was killed in action in 1915.

Chapin, H. C. *Experience of an American Refugee.* Providence, Rhode Island: H. C. Chapin, 1914.

Privately printed.

Chapman, Victor. *Victor Chapman's Letters from France.* New York: Macmillan, 1917.

A vivid picture of the life of a gentleman volunteer is given. The author was a Harvard man who volunteered in the Foreign Legion in 1914, joined the Franco-American Flying Corps (Escadrille), and was shot down over Verdun in 1916.

Chapple, Joseph Mitchell. *We'll Stick to the Finish: C'est la Guerre.* Boston: Chapple, 1918.

The record of the trip to France to observe the progress of the A.E.F.

Christian, Royal A. *Roy's Trip to the Battlefields of Europe.* Chambersburg, Pa.: Kerr, 1918.

A most interesting personal record of a Negro who was the valet to the president of the Cumberland Railroad, and who accompanied his employer to France.

Churchill, Mary Smith. *You Who Can Help.* Boston: Small, Maynard, 1918.

The wife of an American officer stationed in Paris presents a sympathetic picture of wartime France, and appeals to Americans for relief funds.

Churchill, Winston. *A Traveller in War-Time.* New York: Macmillan, 1918.

The author of *The Inside of the Cup* went to Europe shortly after America entered the war, and makes many enthusiastic comments on the character of the Doughboy. The narrative contains an essay, "The American Contribution," in which he credits the United States with making the Great War into a war to save "democracy."

Chute, Arthur Hunt. *Real Help*. New York: Harper, 1918.
A correspondent who joined the Canadian forces in 1914 describes the slaughter, but emphasized the fine character of the individual, Allied soldier.

Clarke, Mrs. M. E. *Paris Waits*, 1914. New York: Putnam, 1915.
An American woman records her impressions of the spirit of Paris as the city awaited the German advance.

Clifton-Shelton, A. *On the Road from Mons*. New York: Dutton, 1917.
A member of the British supply service relates his experiences during the retreat from Mons in 1914.

Cobb, Irvin Shrewsbury. *The Glory of the Coming*. New York: Doran, 1918.
The syndicated newspaper columns of an American correspondent are collected in this narrative; the author is chauvinistic when it comes to the attributes of the A.E.F.

———. *Paths of Glory*. New York: Doran, 1914.
Attached to both the Belgian and German armies early in the conflict, the reporter was most impressed with the awful efficiency of the German army and foresaw, sadly, an eventual German victory. Much maligned for these views, the *Bookman* attacked him by publishing satirical cartoons about him.

———. *Speaking of Prussians*. New York: Doran, 1917.
The reporter relates his front-line experiences and explains why he can no longer be neutral.

Cohen, Israel. *Ruhleben Prison Camp.* New York: Dodd, Mead, 1917.
This is the daily record of an American Jew who was interned in Berlin and later released; rather severe on Germans in general.

Coleman, Frederic. *From Mons to Ypres with French.* New York: Dodd, Mead, 1916.
This is the record of an Englishman who volunteered himself and his automobile in order to drive General French and his staff in the early days of the war. The author is thoroughly romantic, and writes flowery descriptions of the British cavalry.

————.*With Cavalry in the Great War.* Philadelphia: Jacobs, 1917.
This continues the first volume through the second battle of Ypres; the narrator continues to emphasize the romance of the cavalry.

Columban, Dame E. *Irish Nuns at Ypres.* New York: Dutton, 1915.
A story of Germany's brutal invasion of Belgium, this volume also contains the record of how the nuns escaped and found refuge in England.

Copping, Arthur E. *Souls in Khaki.* New York: Doran, 1917.
A Salvation Army official describes his visit to the Front, and expounds on the spiritual beauty of the British soldier.

Corcoran, A. P. *Daredevil of the Army: Experiences as a "Buzzer" and Dispatch Rider.* New York: Dutton, 1918.
A British captain writes a cheaply thrilling account of the signal corps.

Cornet-Anquier, André *Soldier Unafraid.* Boston: Little, Brown, 1918.

This epistolary narrative by a *poilu* on the Alsatian front shows strong faith both in France and in the Cause.

Courtinade, F. *Journal de Guerre d'un Soldat Français*. New York: F. Courtinade, 1916.
Privately printed.

Coyle, Edward Royal. *Ambulancing on the French Front*. New York: Britton, 1918.
An enthusiastic American volunteer at Verdun praises, among other things, the war work of the Y.M.C.A.

Cravath, Paul D. *Great Britain's Part*. New York: Appleton, 1917.
This narrative first appeared in the *New York Times*; the American narrator was given the V.I.P. tour of the British front, and his volume lauds the English soldier, pleads for American preparedness, and predicts the breakdown of German morale.

Crawshay-Williams, Eliot. *Leaves from an Officer's Notebook*. New York: Longmans, 1917.
The narrator traveled from Ypres to Egypt with the B.E.F., and in his narrative states that war is improving the moral fiber of society.

Creighton, Oswin. *With the Twenty-Ninth Division in Gallipoli*. New York: Longmans, 1916.
A Church of England padre with the troops presents a rather pedestrian description of the Dardanelles campaign.

Currie, John Allister. *Red Watch: With the First Canadian Division in Flanders*. New York: Dutton, 1917.
A Canadian colonel writes of the heroism of the 48th Highlanders ("Red Watch") during the blood bath in Flanders.

Curtin, D. Thomas. *The Land of the Deepening Shadow*. New York: Doran, 1917.

An American correspondent in Germany tries to blame all of Germany, not just the Prussians, for the nation's militant aggression.

Cuvru-Mago, Henriette. *Beyond the Marne*, trans. Katharine Babbitt. Boston: Small, Maynard, 1918.
Dedicated to Mildred Aldrich, this narrative is a journal-like record of life near the Marne in August of 1914; contains the stereotyped stories of children's hands being amputated by Germans.

Davis, Richard Harding. *With the Allies*. New York: Scribner's, 1915.
Decidedly pro-Allied, Teddy Roosevelt's ex-press agent wrote this best-seller concerning the early day of the war. Emmett Crozier, in his *American Reporters on the Western Front* (New York, 1959), points out that, in fact, Davis managed to miss most of the war.

————. *With the French in France and Salonika*. New York: Scribner's, 1916.
The most famous of all American combat reporters tries to show that the Great War was just as exciting as was the Spanish-American. Davis toured the war zone and then wrote of French courage and of why and how America should enter the war.

Dawson, Captain A. J. *For France*, illus. by Captain Bruce Bairnsfather. New York: Hodder and Stoughton, 1917.
An English observer with the French army presents an over-done account of the *poilu*, maintaining that there was no unhappiness in the French ranks; this was written after Verdun and the French army mutinies.

Dawson, Conningby William. *Carry-On: Letters in War-Time*. New York: Lane, 1917.
The narrator, Oxford class of '05, became an American citizen before the war. His novels include, *Garden without Walls*

(1913), which was a good seller. He did experience combat, but still believed that war was the best road to a personal, moral renaissance. Best-seller.

————. *Glory of the Trenches*. New York: Lane, 1918.
Contains the same theme as above; also a best-seller.

————. *Out to Win*. New York: Lane, 1918.
The narrator treats the glory of the American forces as well as his previously considered theme.

Dawson, N. P., ed. *Good Soldier: A Selection of Soldiers' Letters, 1914–1918*. New York: Macmillan, 1918.
This is a compilation of "inspirational" letters.

Dearing, V. A. *My Galahad of the Trenches*. New York: Revell, 1918.

Dearmer, Mable. *Letters from a Field Hospital*. New York: Macmillan, 1915.
The writer died of typhus while a hospital worker in Serbia; her sense of dedication is reflected in the letters.

De Gomery, de Gerlache. *Belgium in War Time*, trans. Bernard Miall. New York: Doran, 1916.
Essentially propaganda, this Belgian provides a slanted, but complete, record of German atrocities.

Depew, Albert N. *Gunner Depew*. Chicago: Reilly and Britton, 1918.
This narrative of an American "tough guy" who joined the Foreign Legion is nearly illiterate in presentation, but was popular. There are some particularly scabrous and gory descriptions of trench warfare and of German prison camps.

DeVarila, Osborne. *First Shot of Liberty*. Philadelphia: Winston, 1918.

The narrator claims to have fired the first shot by the A.E.F. at the Germans; he is a teenager, and his style is immature.

DeVille, Father Jean B. *Back from Belgium: A Secret History of Three Years within the German Lines*. New York: Fly, 1918.
An American priest on a mercy mission to Belgium relates the usual atrocity stories.

Dexter, Mary. *In the Soldier's Service*. Boston: Houghton Mifflin, 1918.
An American woman who was first a volunteer nurse in England and then an ambulance driver in France presents a picture of the medical aspects of the war.

Dixon, A. M. *Canteeners*. New York: Dutton, 1918.

Dodd, Anna Bowman. *Heroic France*. New York: Poor, 1915.
A newspaper correspondent, who gives much background on the period just preceding August, 1914, praises the indefatigable spirit of the French.

Dorr, Rheta. *Soldier's Mother in France*. Indianapolis: Bobbs-Merrill, 1918.
An American correspondent in France, who has a son in the A.E.F., writes this narrative to comfort mothers of soldiers.

Doty Madeline Zabriskie. *Behind the Battle Line*. New York: Macmillan, 1918.
On a visit to Russia she sees the chaotic aftermath of the Revolution, much impressed by her visit to noble but suffering France.

——. *Short Rations: An American Woman in Germany*. New York: Century, 1917.
This is an extremely sentimental account of the suffering endured by German women and children during the war.

Downer, Earl Bishop. *Highway of Death*. New York: Davis, 1916.
This is a physician's record of the courageous work done by military hospitals; good observations on wartime life in Belgrade.

Doyle, Sir Arthur Conan. *Visit to Three Fronts*. New York: Doran, 1916.
In this narrative the creator of Sherlock Holmes records his visit to both the Western and Italian fronts, and he expresses his admiration of the fine character of the Allied soldiers.

Drake, Vivian. *Above the Battle*. New York: Appleton, 1918.
This is a record of the Royal Flying Corps, in which the narrator emphasizes the chivalry and excitement inherent in combat flying.

Drumont, Edouard Adolphe. *French Mother in War Time*, trans. Grace E. Bevir. New York: Longmans, 1916.
This reiterates the stock theme of the stoical French faith during a time of suffering.

Dugmore, Radclyfee. *When the Somme Ran Red*. New York: Doran, 1918.
The author, a Captain in the King's Own Yorkshire Light Infantry, was forty-five years old when he volunteered as a second lieutenant. He went because it was a keen adventure for him, and his narrative reflects a definitely nonbitter attitude toward the trench war.

Dunn, Robert. *At the Furthest Front*. New York: Dodd, Mead, 1915.
An American correspondent writes of his trip to the Russian front.

————. *Five Fronts*. New York: Dodd, Mead, 1915.
This narrative includes the correspondent's record of his visit to all of the combat areas, including the Austrian and German lines.

Dupont, Marcel. *In the Field (1914–1915)*, trans. H. W. Hill. Philadelphia: Lippincott, 1916.
A French cavalry officer gives a clear description of trench life, but colors it heavily with religious overtones.

Einstein, Lewis. *Inside Constantinople*. New York: Dutton, 1918.
The narrator was a special agent at the United States Embassy in Constantinople during the Dardanelles Expedition of 1915; his work is designed to show German barbarism, e.g., the Armenian massacres.

Empey, Arthur Guy. *First Call*. New York: Putnam, 1918.
Designed as a guide for the A.E.F., the author includes his own experiences in France so that the green Doughboy might receive some orientation.

————. *"Over the Top," by an American Soldier Who Went*. New York: Putnam, 1917.
This was the most popular of all the narratives, and is still in print. As Putnam's 1917 advertisement states, "His experiences are grim, but they are thrilling and lightened by a touch of humor as original as the *Soldiers Three*. And they are *true*."

————. *Tales from a Dugout*. New York: Century, 1918.
This is a collection of yarns relating the glamour and excitement of life at the front; supposedly, Empey heard all of these stories while in the B.E.F.

Entente Cordial. New York: Ellis, 1918.

Erichsen, Erich. *Forced to Fight: The Tale of a Schleswig Dane*. New York: McBride, 1917.
This is an extremely bitter description of how the Germans forced the narrator to fight in a war which meant nothing to him; describes the pillage of Belgium.

Eydoux-Demians, M. *In a French Hospital,* trans. Betty Yeomans. New York: Duffield, 1915.
The narrator, a French nurse, describes the physical courage and the moral strength of the wounded.

Eye-Witness's Narratives of the War: From the Marne to Neuve Chapelle. New York: Longmans, 1915.
This is a decidedly pro-Allied volume in which are printed the selected writings of official observers.

Fallon, David. *The Big Fight: Gallipoli to the Somme.* New York: Watt, 1918.
The author is an old-line, regimental sergeant-major in the Australian army; although he is extremely patriotic and dedicated to the cause, the narrator relates some of the most gruesome atrocity stories ever published.

Farnam, Ruth. *Nation at Bay: What an American Woman Saw and Did in Suffering Serbia.* Indianapolis: Bobbs-Merrill, 1918.
A volunteer worker relates with much pathos the story of how a small nation was devastated by the Central Powers.

Farrer, Reginald John. *Void of War.* Boston: Houghton Mifflin, 1918.
This is an epistolary narrative in which the author, an American civilian traveling in France and Italy, describes the spiritual apotheosis of the suffering Allied nations.

Flight (pseud.). *Flying Yankee.* New York: Dodd, Mead, 1918.
After his parents were lost on the *Lusitania,* this American joined the Royal Flying Corps to avenge them. He describes the excitement of aerial combat, and is himself something of a rarity, since he survived and returned to New York.

Florez, C. de. *No. 6: A Few Pages from the Diary of an Ambulance Driver.* New York: Dutton, 1918.

This is a record of how an American volunteer's early thirst for excitement turns into a deep feeling for the spirit of France.

Ford, Torrey Sylvester. *Cheer-up Letters from a Private with Pershing*. New York: Clode, 1918.
These letters, from a soldier to his family, are stupidly, inanely cheerful, and are totally out of contact with the war's realities.

Fortescue, Granville Roland. *At the Front with Three Armies*. New York: Brentano, 1915.
An ex-United States army officer turned reporter gives a severe appraisal of the German national character.

————. *France Bears the Burden*. New York: Macmillan, 1917.
This presents virtual encomiums for the *poilu* and for the French nation; contains a particularly descriptive section on Verdun. Some of this material originally appeared in the *Washington Post*.

Fox, Edward Lyell. *Behind the Scenes in Warring Germany*. New York: McBride, 1915.
The author, a "Special Correspondent with the Kaiser's Armies in Berlin," first published this material in the New York *American*. This narrative is unusual because the author is pro-German (although only mildly so), and blames the war on "Lombard Street and John Bull." He excuses the German invasion of Belgium, calls Winston Churchill a "fool," and glorifies von Hindenburg; the book was not notably successful in America.

Frazer, Elizabeth. *Old Glory and Verdun*. New York: Duffield, 1918.
An American volunteer Red Cross and canteen worker in France presents a bubbling and cheerful narrative, and is sad only when picturing the pathetic plight of the refugees.

Fribourg, A. *Flaming Crucible: The Faith of the Fighting Man.* New York: Macmillan, 1918.
The author was a French soldier from 1914 on, and his narrative is a record of how his early thirst for glory turned into a spiritual rebirth that was experienced after he was wounded.

Friends of France; The Field Service of the American Ambulance Described by Its Members. Boston: Houghton Mifflin, 1916.
A romantic account of the Service by a number of its members. ". . . in perishable vision of intrepidity and of heroism as fine as any in the records of knight-errantry or in the annals of Homeric days."

From Dartmouth to the Dardanelles. New York: Dutton, 1917.
An anonymous British naval cadet from the naval academy at Dartmouth, England, records his part in the Gallipoli campaign; his ship was sunk and he was invalided home.

G., H. L. *Meanwhile—A Packet of War Letters.* New York: Dutton, 1916.
These letters were meant to comfort an Englishman on losing a son in the war, and are concerned with the need for patriotic stoicism.

Gaines, Ruth. *A Village in Picardy.* New York: Dutton, 1918.
The narrator was one of a group of Smith College girls who went to France on a "relief" expedition. She is rather patronizing toward the French, and has absolutely no conception of the horrors of the trenches.

Gallishaw, John. *Trenching at Gallipoli: The Personal Narrative of a Newfoundlander.* New York: Century, 1916.
This is the record of a Harvard student who fought the military bureaucracy in order to see combat; he did, and was

wounded. The narrator relates many tales of heroism and is largely uncomplaining of the gross ineptitude that marked the campaign.

Genet, Edmond Charles. *War Letters*. New York: Scribner's, 1918.
The narrator, who first flew with the Franco-American Escadrille, was integrated into the A.E.F. and was the first American flyer to die while flying under American colors. The letters are youthful in tone and record the excitement of flying.

Genevoix, Maurice. *'Neath Verdun: August-October, 1914*, trans. H. Graham Richards. New York: Stokes, 1917.
A French student describes the horror as well as the excitement of the first months of war.

German Deserter's War Experience. New York: Huebsch, 1917.
More than being an anti-German work, this is a socialist tract which registers opposition to all wars as a capitalistic invention.

Gibbons, Floyd. *"And They Thought We Wouldn't Fight."* New York: Doran, 1918.
In many ways, this is the most remarkable narrative to come out of the war. The author was a *Chicago Tribune* correspondent who purposely booked passage on the *Laconia* because of the possibility that it would be torpedoed; it was, and his dispatches helped to push the United States into the war. He writes much on the Adamic American image, and provides an informative record of the early days of the A.E.F. While covering the American participation at Belleau Wood, he lost an eye while accompanying the men into combat. The volume carries a foreword by General Pershing, who cites the author for "playing the game squarely."

Gibbons, Herbert Adams. *Paris Reborn: A Study in Civic Psychology*. New York: Century, 1915.

An American professional travel writer tells how Paris reacted to the German invasion threat; he criticizes French bureaucracy, but praises the French spirit.

Gibbs, Sir Philip H. *The Battles of the Somme.* New York: Doran, 1917.
The author was an officially accredited correspondent with the British and French armies. He rarely saw any actual fighting, and some of his statements are grossly inaccurate. After the war he rushed into print with the brutal *Now It Can Be Told* (1919).

————. *From Baupaume to Passchendaele.* New York: Doran, 1918.
This is a detailed history of the hell of Arras and the Somme, written in the form of daily dispatches.

————. *The Soul of the War.* New York: McBride, 1918.
First published in England, in 1915. This narrative is mainly concerned with the heroism of the "Old Contemptibles," i.e., the British professional soldiers of 1914.

Gibson, Preston. *Battering the Boche.* New York: Century, 1918.
By an American volunteer in the Norton-Harjes Corps, this narrative carries a foreword by a United States Marine Corps general who praises it as an "incentive and example" to American soldiers.

Gilliland, H. G. *My German Prisons.* New York: Hodder and Stoughton, 1918.
Since this book is dedicated to Ambassador James Gerrard, it was obviously written for American consumption. The British soldier-narrator includes many atrocity stories of Germans bayoneting the wounded, and presents a rather sordid picture of a soldier's lot in German prisons.

Giraudoux, Jean. *Campaigns and Intervals.* Boston: Houghton Mifflin, 1918.

A French novelist turned soldier writes some restrained combat descriptions, but he does not doubt the righteousness of the cause.

Gleason, Arthur H. *Our Part in the Great War*. New York: Burt, 1917.
The author went to Europe with the blessings of Teddy Roosevelt, and his narrative both praises the valor of American volunteers and campaigns for American entry into the conflict; neutrality is referred to as, ". . . this reveling in fat money vaults."

————. *With the First War Ambulances in Belgium*. New York: Burt, 1918.
As in the previous narrative, the author glorifies the Americans who volunteered to fight before America became officially involved.

————. *Young Hilda at the Wars*. New York: Stokes, 1915.
This is a slight fictionalization of the events connected with his volunteer work with the Belgian Red Cross; he relates the usual tales of Belgian bravery.

Gleason, Arthur H., and Helen Hays. *Golden Lads*. New York: Century, 1916.
This contains an introduction by Teddy Roosevelt, and relates experiences undergone while the narrator served in the Belgian ambulance service. There is a categorical condemnation of everything German.

Gomez-Carrillo, Énrique. *Among the Ruins*, trans. Florence Simmonds. New York: Doran, 1916.
A Spanish journalist describes the horrors of war, and particularly the German atrocities. For a "neutral," he is strongly pro-Allied.

————. *In the Heart of the Tragedy*. New York: Hodder and Stoughton, 1917.
A continuation of the above.

Grant, Reginald. *S.O.S. Stand To!* New York: Appleton, 1918.

The author volunteered for the 1st Canadian Division in 1914, and had the almost incredible luck to survive the entire Somme, Vimy Ridge, and other campaigns without mishap, although his unit suffered 60 per cent killed. He was fascinated by trench life, and he presents a vigorous and detailed account of it.

Grant, Robert. *Their Spirit: Some Impressions of the English and French during the Summer of 1916.* Boston: Houghton Mifflin, 1916.

The narrator was a reporter for the *Boston Evening Transcript* who visited the Western Front. He writes much on the glorious spirit of the soldiers, and is strongly in favor of American intervention.

Grasty, Charles H. *Flashes from the Front.* New York: Century, 1918.

This volume, by a war correspondent for the *New York Times*, carries an introduction and recommendation by General Pershing. The author was possessed with the excitement of war, and describes a battle scene as "indescribably wonderful."

Green, Horace. *Log of a Non-Combatant.* Boston: Houghton Mifflin, 1915.

An American journalist presents his impressions of the bombardment of Antwerp, although he does try to deemphasize stories of German atrocities.

Grondys, L. H. *Germans in Belgium.* New York: Appleton, 1916.

A Dutch professor travels to Belgium to verify the stories of German atrocities; he is convinced.

Grow, Malcolm Cummings. *Surgeon Grow: American in the Russian Fighting.* New York: Stokes, 1918.

Writing after the Russian Revolution, the author tries to enlist aid for Russia in order to give it stability. He actually saw combat service, and his unintended descriptions of Russian leadership and logistics help one to understand some of the causes of the Revolution.

Haigh, Richard. *Life in a Tank*. Boston: Houghton Mifflin, 1918.

A British infantry captain who saw action on the Somme with the tanks writes a matter-of-fact description of this hazardous new duty.

Hale, Walter. *By Motor to the Firing Line*. New York: Century, 1916.

First appearing in *Collier's*, this light narrative was written by an American illustrator who toured the battle line.

Hall, Bert. *En l'air!* New York: New Library, 1918.

This is the record of an American volunteer who volunteered in the Foreign Legion, transferred to the Lafayette Escadrille, and witnessed part of the Russian Revolution.

Hall, James Norman. *High Adventure*. New York: Burt, 1917.

A Harvard man who flew Spads in the Lafayette Escadrille presents an absorbing and well-written account of his life. While not chauvinistic, the narrative does emphasize the adventure and personal thrill of air combat.

———. *Kitchener's Mob: The Adventures of an American with the British Army*. Boston: Atlantic Monthly Company, 1916.

This best-seller concerns the author's early war career, during which time he fought with the British "New Armies" on the Somme. He is an anglophile who feels that Tommy Atkins is the greatest, most stoical soldier of all.

Hall, Jan [John Beith]. *All In It*. New York: Doubleday, 1917.

This best-seller was the second volume of the author's series
In describing his part in the Ypres action, he shows a sort
of amused condescension toward it all, and looks at war as
a good-humored adventure.

————. *The First Hundred Thousand.* New York: Grosset
and Dunlap, 1917.
This was originally an anonymous narrative in *Blackwood's
Magazine*, was reprinted and became a best-seller in America.
The author describes his activities as a captain in the Argyll
and Sutherland Highlanders in France.

————. *Getting Together.* New York: Doubleday, 1917.
The narrator's first two books proved so popular that the
British government sent him on a special propaganda mission
to America. The narrator tries to answer popular American
"misconceptions" concerning England and her allies.

Hankey, Donald. *A Student in Arms.* New York: Dutton,
1917.
The author of this best-seller died *à guerre* after this was
written. He admits that war "brutalizes" soldiers, but also
writes chapters on "The Good Side of Militarism," and "Romance." Hankey is quite perceptive about men's emotions,
and is far from being a hack writer.

Hargrave, John. *At Sulva Bay.* Boston: Houghton Mifflin,
1917.
The English narrator, a professional writer and author who
enlisted in the B.E.F., describes men's lives during the Dardanelles campaign.

Harvey, Harold. *A Soldier's Sketches Under Fire.* New York:
Allen, 1916.
This volume contains a professional illustrator's record of the
good-humored fellowship enjoyed by the British soldiers early
in the war; he was gassed and wounded in action.

Hayes, Ralph A. *Secretary Baker at the Front*. New York: Century, 1918.

The narrator was private secretary to Secretary of War Baker from February to April, 1918.

Heath, Arthur George. *Letters of Arthur George Heath, Fellow of New College, Oxford, and Lieutenant in the 6th Battalion, Royal West Kent Regiment*. New York: Longmans, 1917.

The twenty-eight-year-old scholar shows a quiet sense of dedication in his letters; he was killed in action.

Hewett, S. A. *Scholar's Letters from the Front*. New York: Longmans, 1918.

Hoggson, Noble Foster. *Just Behind the Front in France*. New York: Lane, 1918.

A member of the United States Industrial Commission that visited France in 1918 records some of the pathos of civilian suffering.

Holmes, R. Derby. *A Yankee in the Trenches*. Boston: Little, Brown, 1918.

The narrator was a volunteer corporal in the 22nd London Battalion of the Queen's Royal West Surrey Regiment. Wounded and discharged, he writes in much the same style as Sergeant Empey, in order to "awake the American people to the dangers of Prussianism."

Hopkins, Nevil Monroe. *Over the Threshold of War*. Philadelphia: Lippincott, 1918.

The author, a writer of mystery novels, depicts the early days in France when he worked at the American Embassy. He was present at Mons and his appraisal is rather objective, but he does relate the usual stories of German atrocities.

Howard, F. *On Three Battle Fronts*. New York: Vechten-Warring, 1918.
This is a limited subscription edition.

Howe, Mark Anthony De Wolfe, ed. *The Harvard Volunteers in Europe*. Cambridge, Mass.: Harvard University Press, 1916.
By 1916, twenty Harvard men had died in the Great War, and five had perished on the *Lusitania*. These letters show the spirit of romance and excitement in which the collegians went to war; there are some feeble attempts at neutrality, but the "blood" ties of England and New England are evident.

Huard, Francis Wilson. *My Home in the Field of Honor*. New York: Doran, 1917.
This best-seller was the first in a series of narratives in which the author describes her life at a French village in the path of the German advance.

———. *My Home in the Field of Mercy*. New York: Doran, 1917.
In her second volume the narrator describes how she made her château into a makeshift hospital for the French wounded. Although the volume is intelligent and well written, it does include such emotional appeals as accusations that the Germans raped French children; a best-seller.

———. *With Those Who Wait*. New York: Doran, 1918.
The final volume of the series treats the suffering of the women and old men who wait at home while their sons fight and die.

Hunt, Edward Eyre. *War Bread*. New York: Holt, 1916.
A record of Belgian suffering by a member of the American Commission for Relief in Belgium.

Hurst, G. B. *With Manchesters in the East*. New York: Longmans, 1918.

Imbrie, Robert Whitney. *Behind the Wheel of a War Ambulance*. New York: McBride, 1918.
This is a volunteer's record of his experiences from the Aisne to the Balkans; rather modest in tone.

Irwin, William Henry. *Latin at War*. New York: Appleton, 1917.
An American observer writes enthusiastically about the democratic qualities of the French, and about the admirable, soldierly qualities of the Italians and the French.

————. *Men, Women, and War*. New York: Appleton, 1915.
Completely pro-Allied, the narrator writes on the theme of democracy at war, and portrays the suffering of innocent French and Belgian women.

————. *Reporter at Armageddon*. New York: Appleton, 1918.
With the French troops, and later with the Americans, this correspondent's letters vividly portray what he considers to be the glory of the Cause.

Jeffries, J. *War Diary of an American Woman to the Proclamation of the Holy War*. New York: Fatherland Press, 1915.

Jenkins, Burris A. *Facing the Hindenburg Line*. New York: Revell, 1917.
This volume contains the impressions of an observer with the B.E.F. He had no combat experience, but he did get to fly, and compared combat aviation with chivalry.

Johnson, E. A. *Torpedoed in the Mediterranean*. New York: Ogilive, 1918.

Johnson, Owen McMahon. *Spirit of France*. Boston: Little, Brown, 1916.

An American on a V.I.P. tour of the French lines writes an extended comparison between the mechanistic, autocratic Germans, and the individualistic, democratic French.

Jones, W. *Fighting the Hun from Saddle and Trench.* New York: Aiken, 1918.

Juvenis (pseud.). *Sulva Bay and After.* New York: Hodder and Stoughton, 1916.
This narrative is written in a scholarly manner (the author compares the Sulva Bay expedition to that of the Athenians at Syracuse), and contains a detailed description of British "muddling through."

Kauffman, Reginald Wright. *In a Moment of Time: Things Seen on the Bread-Line of Belgium.* New York: Moffat, 1915.
A civilian observes, with much pathos, the devastation wrought by the Germans in Belgium.

Kautz, John Iden. *Trucking to the Trenches.* Boston: Houghton Mifflin, 1918.
The narrator was too young for service with the A.E.F., so he volunteered as a French camion driver; epistolary in form, the volume reflects a spirit of youthful adventure.

Keeling, Frederic. *Keeling Letters and Recollections.* New York: Macmillan, 1918.
An early leader of the Fabian Society at Cambridge writes to his family and friends; his patriotism overshadows his sociopolitical beliefs. Cited for gallantry in action, he died on the Somme in 1916.

Keene, Louis. *"Crumps": The Plain Story of a Canadian Who Went.* Boston: Houghton Mifflin, 1917.
This contains a preface by General Leonard Wood, who advocates "Preparedness." The narrator enlisted in 1914 and

became a subaltern in charge of a machine-gun section. His patriotic and determined attitude is not dampened by the fact that he lost a hand near Ypres; he was an artist before the war.

Kehoe, Thomas Joseph. *Fighting Mascot*. New York: Dodd, Mead, 1918.
This Englishman was so young when he enlisted that he was almost the battalion mascot. He was excited and thrilled by war, even though he was wounded and invalided home.

Kelly, Russell Anthony. *Kelly of the Foreign Legion*. New York: Kennerley, 1917.
The letters of this American volunteer show that he realizes the absurdity of war, but also express how he gloried in its excitement. He was killed in 1916.

Kennard, Dorothy Katherine. *Roumanian Diary*. New York: Dodd, Mead, 1918.
This is a description of the havoc caused by Roumania's entry into the war; some of the descriptions of the suffering civilians are quite vivid.

Kipling, Rudyard. *France at War: On the Frontier of Civilization*. New York: Doubleday, 1915.
In his usual, romantic manner, the chronicler of the British army gives an extremely subjective impression on the worthiness of the grand cause. Best-seller.

Klein, Felix. *Hope in Suffering: Diary of a French Army Chaplain*. Chicago: McClurg, 1917.
Writing in an extremely patriotic manner, the priest treats the spiritual and moral fulfillment of broken men.

Knyvett, R. Hugh. *"Over the Top" with the Australians*. New York: Scribner's, 1918.
The narrator, an Anzac captain, saw action at Gallipoli and the Somme. The heroism and fighting qualities of the Adamic

men from down under are treated in an extremely romantic manner. The horror of war is described but a sense of excitement permeates all, and frequent quotes from Robert W. Service emphasize that war is a virile game.

Kreisler, Fritz. *Four Weeks in the Trenches: The War Story of a Violinist.* Boston: Houghton Mifflin, 1915.
This best-seller is most unusual because it shows how an essentially aesthetic person could be so caught up in the romantic spirit of the war that he could join his regiment and enjoy it thoroughly. The narrative appeared early enough in the war so that Americans did not feel compelled to criticize Kreisler for fighting for Austria; too, the narrative is adventuresome, not chauvinistic in tone.

L., R. A. *Letters of Canadian Stretcher Bearer.* Boston: Little, 1918.

Lafond, George. *Covered with Mud and Glory.* Boston: Small, Maynard, 1918.
The narrator, a French machine-gun sergeant, writes in a vivid, straightforward manner, describing the awful slaughter, but coloring his stories with tints of glory.

Lake, Harold. *Campaigning in the Balkans.* New York: McBride, 1918.
The record of an English lieutenant during the Macedonian campaign; rather dully professional.

LaMotte, Ellen N. *The Backwash of War.* New York: Putnam, 1916.
By any standard, this is the most bitterly disillusioned of all of the 1914–1918 narratives; in fact, it resembles William March's *Company K.* more than it does the narratives written during the war. Although the author admits to the glory of war, she states that her book should serve to balance the books that romanticize war. Humanity is all rotten, soldiers smell, French wives are "ugly," and French and Belgian

women become whores mainly out of silly amusement. France and England prohibited the sale of the volume, and the United States banned it after her entry into the war.

Lapradelle, Albert Geouffre de, and Frederic René Coudert, eds. *War Letters from France.* Chicago: McClurg, 1916. These are letters which were selected to show the glorious, romantic spirit of France.

Lardner, Ring W. *My Four Weeks in France.* Indianapolis: Bobbs-Merrill, 1918.
This famous humorist writes a light account of his abortive trip to France and England; mainly, it concerns his difficulties with the French bureaucracy.

Lauder, Harry. *A Minstrel in France.* New York: Hearst, 1918.
The author, probably the most famous Scotch singer of all time, toured the front to cheer the troops after losing a son who died fighting with a Highland regiment. His narrative is a record of this trip, and also mentions his tour of America; exceedingly romantic in regards to the cause.

Lauler, M. R. *My Personal Experiences in Belgium and France.* Indianapolis: French Orphans' Guard, 1918.

Le Guiner, Jeanne. *Letters from France,* trans. H. M. C. Boston: Houghton Mifflin, 1916.
The author was a Franco-American student at the Sorbonne, and her letters depict the atmosphere of wartime Paris.

LeRoux, Robert Charles. *On the Field of Honor.* Boston: Houghton Mifflin, 1918.
This narrative follows the experiences of a French lieutenant through his letters. It is full of pathos and suffering, but it shows a spirit of sacrifice which is necessary so that France might live.

Lettres de Mon Soldat, 1915–1916. New York: Neeser, 1916.

Liddell, Robert Scotland. *Actions and Reactions in Russia.* New York: Dutton, 1918.
An Englishman who served in the Russian army writes some interesting descriptions of the war against Germany and of the Revolution.

Lintier, P. *My .75: Reminiscences of a Gunner of a .75 m/m Battery in 1914.* New York: Doran, 1917.
Contains a preface by Francis Huard. The author, who was killed in action, writes of the fine, eager enthusiasm and patriotism that was particularly in evidence during the early months of the war.

Lister, Charles Alfred. *Charles Lister: Letters and Recollections.* New York: Scribner's, 1917.
These are the educated writings of Lord Ribblesdale's son, who was killed in the Gallipoli action.

Liveing, Edward George Downing. *Attack.* New York: Macmillan, 1918.
This has a preface by John Masefield. Wounded on the Somme, the author is realistic enough to display his feelings of fear and confusion during the attack, but does not express a bitterness toward the war.

Livingston, St. Clair and Ingeborg Steen-Hansen. *Under Three Flags.* New York: Macmillan, 1916.
The narrators, two American nurses who were living in Paris, volunteered for Red Cross duty in France, Belgium and Serbia; the narrative is not blatantly patriotic, but is definitely pro-Allied.

Lodge, Sir Oliver Joseph. *Raymond; or, Life and Death.* New York: Doran, 1916.

In perhaps the strangest of the narratives, the scientist-author claims to have presented a record of psychic conversations with his son, who was killed in action.

Long, Robert Edward Crozier. *Colours of War*. New York: Scribner's, 1915.
The American observer who narrates this volume tries to be fair in his portrayal of the Eastern Front, but he shows much sympathy for the Russians.

Loti, Pierre [Julien Viaud]. *War*, trans. Marjorie Laurie. Philadelphia: Lippincott, 1917.
This is a French naval reservist's record of 1914–1915. Admittedly slanted toward neutral nations, this narrative is a collection of combat stories which emphasize the bravery of the French and Belgians and the barbarism of the Germans.

McBride, Herbert W. *Emma Gees*. Indianapolis: Bobbs-Merrill, 1918.
A machine gunner with the 21st Canadian Infantry presents an extremely vivid account of his combat. The narrative is not sentimental in tone, but it contains many thrilling exploits.

McClintock, A. *Best o' Luck*. New York: Grosset and Dunlap, 1917.

McClurg, Nellie Letitia. *Three Times and Out, Told by Private Limmons*. Boston: Houghton Mifflin, 1918.
The author tells of a Canadian private's experiences in escaping from a German prisoner-of-war camp.

McConnell, James R. *Flying for France*. New York: Doubleday, 1917.
An American volunteer with the Lafayette Escadrille writes an enthusiastic narrative on the chivalry and excitement of the air war.

McCormick, Robert R. *With the Russian Army, Being the Experiences of a National Guardsman.* New York: Macmillan, 1915.

The narrator, who was to become the famous editor of the *Chicago Tribune*, was the son of a former American ambassador to Russia. He looks at Wilson and America's lack of preparedness as something of a dark plot, and praises the cult of individualism and the active life of a soldier.

McCoy, Patrick Terrance (pseud.). *Kiltie McCoy.* Indianapolis: Bobbs–Merrill, 1918.

The narrator, an Irish-American fighting with a Highland regiment in France, enlisted in 1914, was wounded and discharged. His descriptions of army life are detailed and varied.

McDougal, Grace. *Nurse at the War.* New York: McBride, 1917.

This is a light story of an American nurse at the Western Front; she appears to be more interested in woman's emancipation than in the wounded.

MacGill, Patrick. *Great Push: An Episode of the Great War.* New York: Doran, 1916.

A British soldier describes the death machine of the Somme; this narrative is positive in tone only when depicting the courage of the men.

————. *Red Horizon.* New York: Doran, 1916.

The first of the two narratives, this is far lighter in tone than the above because it reflects the bouyancy of Kitchener's "New Armies," yet unbloodied at the Somme.

Mack, Arthur James. *Shellproof Mack.* Boston: Small, Maynard, 1918.

The author was an American with the British forces. After he was wounded and sent home, he wrote this extremely vernacular narrative.

Mackay, Helen Gansevoort. *Journal of Small Things*. New York: Duffield, 1917.
An American woman writes a rather inane journal on the beauty of the French soul.

McMullen, Fred, and Jack Evans. *Out of the Jaws of Hunland*. New York: Putnam, 1918.
Written by two Canadians who escaped from a German prisoner-of-war camp, this narrative contains some revealing observations on the severe economic straits of Germany.

McNair, Wilson. *Blood and Iron*. New York: Dutton, 1916.
The author, a British civilian, treats the war romantically, including exciting descriptions of cavalry and admiring portrayals of "brave Belgians." There is an extensive description of the first battle of the Marne.

Macnaughtan, Sarah. *Woman's Diary of the War*. New York: Dutton, 1916.
A writer of popular novels, the narrator tells of her experiences with the Red Cross in Belgium.

MacQuarrie, Hector. *How to Live at the Front*. Philadelphia: Lippincott, 1917.
A British lieutenant in the Royal Field Artillery tells his combat experiences for the benefit of the Americans going Over There. He presents a rather pragmatic picture of trench life, but he does emphasize the necessity for spiritual preparation of the soldiers.

———. *Over Here: Impressions of America by a British Officer*. Philadelphia: Lippincott, 1918.
Sent to America as an inspector of artillery production, the narrator tells some of his combat experiences, but mainly provides a fascinating travel description of America.

Malcolm, Ian Zachary. *War Pictures Behind the Lines*. New York: Dutton, 1915.

The author presents a common picture of Red Cross work in France.

Malherbe, Henry. *The Flame That is France.* New York: Century, 1918.

The French version of this narrative (*La Flamme au Poing*) won the French Academy award for 1917. Although philosophically and aesthetically opposed to all war, the narrator sees the French cause as just and worthy.

Mallet, Christian. *Impressions and Experiences of a French Trooper.* New York: Dutton, 1916.

Although the narrator does realistically describe his fears of combat, his comments serve to underline the popular picture of the indominable spirit of France.

Manion, Robert J. *Surgeon in Arms.* New York: Appleton, 1918.

A Canadian MD at the Front writes more on trench life than on hospitals; his style is uncultivated.

Manwaring, G. B. *If We Return: Letters of a Soldier of Kitchener's Army.* New York: Lane, 1918.

Epistolary in form, this volume contains the comments of educated English officers, and imparts the feeling that war is somehow unreal.

Martin, Arthur Anderson. *Surgeon in Khaki.* New York: Longmans, 1915.

A New Zealand surgeon with the B.E.F. glorifies the famous retreat from Mons in 1914.

Masefield, John. *Gallipoli.* New York: Grosset and Dunlap, 1916.

Long hailed as the best written of all the war narratives, this volume contains the Poet Laureate's record of the Dardanelles campaign. It is a complete military history of the campaign, not merely a record of his own part in it, and attempts to apologize for the debacle.

Merrill, Wainwright. *A College Man in Khaki: Letters of an American in the British Artillery.* New York: Doran, 1918. The author, who was to have been graduated from Harvard in 1919, volunteered with the C.E.F. and was killed at Ypres. He is extremely romantic in orientation, even lauding Mary Shipman Andrews, and the Great War was for him a pilgrimage to save his beloved England.

Miller, Francis Trevelyan, ed. *True Stories of the Great War.* 6 Vols. New York: Review of Reviews, 1918. This is an anthology of narratives, all of which are luridly romantic. The stories were taken from books, periodicals and newspapers.

Millet, Phillippe. *Comrades in Arms,* trans. Lady Frazer. New York: Doran, 1917. A French liaison officer with the British forces emphasizes the spirit of brotherhood that he claims exists between the two armies.

Milne, James. *News from "Somewhere."* New York: Putnam, 1916. This is composed of a series of romantic sketches of England at war.

Mitchell, Frederick. *Fred Mitchell's War Story: Three Years in the War Zone.* New York: Knopf, 1918. An English jockey caught in France tries to convey to the American reader the privations of the refugees.

More Letters from Billy. New York: Doran, 1917.

Morgan, John Hartman. *Leaves from a Field Note-Book.* New York: Macmillan, 1916.

A British observer presents a lighthearted portrayal of Tommy Atkin's character.

Morgenthau, Henry. *Ambassador Morgenthau's Story.* New York: Doubleday, 1918.
Published in England as *Secrets of the Bosphorus*, this narrative by the former American ambassador to Turkey points to the German-Turkish plot, and to the fact that most Turks despised the Germans.

Morlae, Edward. *Soldier of the Legion.* Boston: Houghton Mifflin, 1916.
Reprinted from the *Atlantic Monthly*, this narrative relates the exploits of an American volunteer in the Foreign Legion.

Morse, John. *In the Russian Ranks.* New York: Knopf, 1916.
An Englishman gives "eyewitness" accounts of German barbarism; he has high praise for the fighting qualities of Russian troops.

————. *In the French Ranks.* New York: Grosset and Dunlap, 1918.
The narrative is essentially the same in style and approach as the above, but takes place on the Western Front.

Mortimer, Maud. *Green Tent in Flanders.* New York: Doubleday, 1917.
An American volunteer nurse presents a sympathetic and sentimental picture of the wounded.

Mucke, Hellmath von. *Ayesha.* Boston: Ritter, 1917.
This is the record of a "gentlemanly" German sea raider; since he was chivalrous and did not sink ships without warning, his exciting exploits made acceptable reading for Americans.

————. *The Emden.* Boston: Ritter, 1917.
This is an expansion of the above.

Muhlon, Wilhelm. *Vandals of Europe*, trans. N. L. McPherson. New York: Putnam, 1918.
Disturbed over the nature of German foreign policy and internal corruption, a German director of Krupp allowed his highly critical diary to be published.

Munroe, J. *Mopping Up*. New York: Fly, 1918.

Musgrave, George Clark. *Under Four Flags for France*. New York: Appleton, 1918.
An American reporter writes a highly pro-Allied account of the war; general in scope, it does include a record of his personal experiences while visiting the Western Front before America's entry into the war.

My Secret Service. New York: Doran, 1916.
By "the man who dined with the Kaiser," this is the record of an American "neutral" who was hired by the *London Daily Mail* to report on Germany.

Nasmith, George Gallie. *On the Fringe of the Great Fight*. New York: Doran, 1918.
A British medical officer in France, who, incidentally, invented the gas mask, makes some interesting remarks on the sanitation and health problems of the war.

Neil, H. *Exciting Personal Experiences: Europe at War*. New York: Bible House, 1914.
Unavailable, but since it was published by Bible House, one can guess at the nature of its content.

Nicolas, Sous-Lieutenant René. *Campaign Diary of a French Officer*, trans. Katharine Babbitt. Boston: Houghton Mifflin, 1917.
The author published this in answer to the "many questions" that he was asked during his American tour. Wounded in action, he was still much impressed by the romantic trap-

pings of war, and his narrative contains a vivid description of how he felt during a frenzied charge.

Nobbs, Captain Gilbert. *On the Right of the British Line.* New York: Scribner's, 1917.
A young Territorial officer records his trip to France and the battle of the Somme. Although he was shot through the eyes and rendered blind, he shows absolutely no bitterness, even though only six men out of his two-hundred-man company survived.

Northcliffe, Lord. *Lord Northcliffe's War Book.* New York: Doran, 1917.
The author, publisher of the *London Times*, wrote this especially for American consumption; high praise is given to American volunteers and to the first soldiers of the A.E.F.

O'Brien, Lieutenant Pat. *Outwitting the Hun: My Escape from a German Prison Camp.* New York: Harper, 1918.
A United States citizen who enlisted with the Royal Flying Corps in Canada, the narrator was shot down and captured by the Germans. His escape to Holland is really an incredible and intensely romantic story, which makes one of the most interesting and readable narratives of the war.

Odell, Joseph H. *The New Spirit of the New Army: A Message to "Service Flag" Homes.* New York: Revell, 1918.
An euphoric narrative on American soldiers and the "Christian" camp life in the United States, it was written to assure mothers that their sons were not being led straight to sin and damnation.

Ogilvie, F. B., ed. *Stories and Letters from the Trenches.* New York: Ogilvie, 1915.

Orcutt, Philip Dana. *White Road of Mystery.* New York: Lane, 1918.

An American volunteer ambulance driver in France presents an introspective, personal record of his war experiences.

O'Shaughnessy, Edith. *My Lorraine Journal.* New York: Harper, 1918.
The narrator is an American woman who did some canteen work in France, but who mainly had a "nice" tour of the battlefields; she includes a romantic description of Verdun.

Oxenham, John. *High Altars.* New York: Doran, 1918.
A civilian observer at the Western Front writes of the Christian uplift and spiritual revival of the troops.

Palmer, Frederic. *America in France.* New York: Dodd, Mead, 1918.
The Chief Press Officer of the A.E.F. writes a full description of America's part in the Great War; extremely enthusiastic and chauvinistic.

————. *My Second Year of the War.* New York: Dodd, Mead, 1917.
Essentially romantic in orientation, the author describes the "Big Push" on the Somme and pushes for American intervention.

————. *My Third Year of the War.* New York: Burt, 1918.
A continuation of the above.

————. *My Year of the Great War.* New York: Dodd, Mead, 1915.
Although an American, the narrator makes no pretense at being neutral; "Between right and wrong one cannot be a neutral." In addition to visiting France, he visited Germany and found little to recommend it.

Pares, Bernard. *Day by Day with the Russian Army.* Boston: Houghton Mifflin, 1915.

An English attaché to the Russian forces emphasizes the fighting qualities of the Russian soldier, and tries to portray the Russian army as being democratic.

Patterson, John Henry. *With the Zionists in Gallipoli.* New York: Doran, 1916.
This is the rather factual account of the Zionist mule corps which saw action at Gallipoli.

Patterson, Joseph Medill. *Notebook of a Neutral.* New York: Duffield, 1915.
The narrative first appeared in the *Chicago Tribune*, and is the chauvinistic record of an American abroad; in favor of intervention.

Payne, J. L. *What I Saw in England and France.* Brooklyn: Brooklyn Daily Eagle Press, 1916.

Pearson, George Eustace. *Escape of a Princess Pat.* New York: Doran, 1918.
The author pieces together the diary of Corporal Edwards of Canada and tells the story of his escape from a German prison camp.

Peat, Harold. *Private Peat.* Indianapolis: Bobbs-Merrill, 1917.
Next to Sergeant Empey's *Over the Top*, this is probably the most popular narrative of the war. The author enlisted in the Canadian forces, was wounded in combat, and sent home; he relates many exciting adventures in which he participated.

Peat, Louisa Watson. *Mrs. Private Peat.* Indianapolis: Bobbs-Merrill, 1918.
So great was the fame of her husband that she capitalized on it to produce this badly done monument to English womanhood.

Pinkerton, R. Douglas. *"Ladies from Hell."* New York: Century, 1918.
A sergeant in the London Scottish wrote this in order to tell Americans something of the excitement and romance of war.

Poling, Daniel Alfred. *Hats in Hell.* Boston: Christian Endeavor World, 1918.
This narrative is a record of the work of its minister author in the Y.M.C.A. huts in France.

Porter, William Townsend. *Shock at the Front.* Boston: Atlantic Monthly Press, 1918.
The narrator was an American surgeon who traveled to France to help with the wounded and to study the effects of shock on the wounded.

Powell, E. Alexander. *Italy at War.* New York: Scribner's, 1917.
A correspondent for the *New York World* and later a captain in the A.E.F., the author traveled to Italy to report on the "forgotten war," which he found to be romantic in its Alpine setting.

————.*Vive la France.* New York: Scribner's, 1915.
In this volume the narrator reports on the V.I.P. tour which he was given of France; he naïvely assumed that he witnessed typical combat conditions.

Price, Julius Mendes. *Six Months on the Italian Front.* New York: Dutton, 1917.
An English war correspondent records the fine fighting qualities of the Italians, as well as the barbarism of the Austrians.

Prince, Norman. *A Volunteer Who Died for the Cause He Loved.* Boston: Houghton Mifflin, 1917.
Epistolary in form, this narrative records the exploits of a cum laude Harvard graduate who enlisted in the Lafayette

Escadrille, had nine kills and became our first ace, and was killed in action.

Pulitzer, R. *Over the Front in an Aeroplane.* New York: Harper, 1915.
An American observer in France tells of his adventures in aviation, and also attempts to give the "definitive" answer on why the Germans did not reach Paris in 1914.

Rae, Herbert (pseud.). *Maple Leaves in Flanders Fields.* New York: Dutton, 1917.
Writing in a light and witty manner of his service in the C.E.F., the narrator is far more concerned with the good humor of the soldiers than with the war itself.

Redier, Antoine. *Comrades in Courage,* trans. Mrs. Philip Duncan Wilson. New York: Doubleday, 1918.
A French lieutenant in describing his combat career eulogizes France, Motherhood, Chivalry and Duty.

Redmond, William. *Trench Pictures from France.* New York: Doran, 1918.
The narrator, later killed in France, was a major who was an Irish MP and champion of Irish independence; at fifty-four years old, he was the first one over the top in the Somme push. He emphasizes the resurgence of religion due to the war.

Reed, John. *The War in Eastern Europe.* New York: Scribner's, 1916.
Most famous for his *Ten Days that Shook the World,* the author of this narrative presents a picture of the plague areas of Serbia. His descriptions of his Russian visit are most interesting, especially because he founded the Communist Party in America.

Rice, P. S. *American Crusader at Verdun.* Princeton: Rice, 1918.
Privately printed.

Richthofen, Captain Manfred Freiberr von. *The Red Battle Flyer*, trans. J. Ellis Barker. New York: McBride, 1918.
The narrator was the famous leader of the Flying Circus; the narrative is carefully censored, but it does show the narrator as a young aristocrat who was fascinated by the excitement of the air. Since the author was an unregenerate German, the volume contains a preface justifying its publication in America; it is maintained that the Baron is chivalrous and not a Hun.

Riggs, Arthur Stanley. *With Three Armies on and behind the Western Front*. Indianapolis: Bobbs-Merrill, 1918.
An American civilian centers most of his praise on the A.E.F., and writes encomiums on the character of the Adamic American.

Rinehart, Mary Roberts. *Kings, Queens and Pawns*. New York: Doran, 1915.
Abandoning her writing of detective novels long enough to tour hospitals on the Western Front, this American tries feebly to maintain a cloak of neutrality, but admits, "I hold a strong brief for the English. . . ."

Roberts, Lieutenant E. M. *A Flying Fighter: An American above the Lines in France*. New York: Harper, 1918.
The avowed purpose of the book is to educate America on the war. The narrator, a born adventurer and friend of Jack London, enlisted in the British infantry in 1914, transferred to the Royal Flying Service, shot down seven German planes and was wounded four times. Although the writing is quite sophomoric and quite romantic, the book does contain a fine description of aerial combat.

Robinson, Harry Perry. *Turning Point: The Battle of the Somme*. New York: Dodd, Mead, 1917.
A correspondent for the London *Times* tells of the slaughter of the Somme without dwelling on the details of the awful butchery; optimistic in tone.

Robinson, William J. *My Fourteen Months at the Front: An American Boy's Baptism of Fire*. Boston: Little, Brown, 1916.
The narrator volunteered in the Dragoon Guards as an adventure, and took part in the landings at Ostend early in the war. Although juvenile in prose style, the narrative does provide an interesting picture of the confused early days of the war.

Root, Esther Sayles, and Marjorie Crocker. *Over Periscope Pond: Letters from Two American Girls in Paris, October, 1916–January, 1918*. Boston: Houghton Mifflin, 1918.
The authors seem to have had a fine adventure by engaging in refugee relief work; quite patronizing to the refugees and to the wounded *poilus*.

Rosher, Harold. *With the Flying Squadron*. New York: Macmillan, 1916.
The letters of a young aviator, later killed, glowingly describe the excitement that he found in flying for the Royal Navy.

Rossiter, Ivan. *In Kultured Kaptivity*. Indianapolis: Bobbs-Merrill, 1918.
A record of German prison-camp barbarism by a captured member of the First Canadian Mounted Rifles.

Ruhl, Arthur. *Antwerp to Gallipoli*. New York: Scribner's, 1916.
Staunchly pro-Allied, the author was an American reporter who visited France, Belgium, England, and Germany. He was impressed by German efficiency, but believed in the Allied cause.

Rutledge, S. *Pen Pictures from the Trenches*. New York: Briggs, 1918.

Seeger, Alan. *Letters and Diary*. New York: Scribner's, 1917.
This Harvard poet was one of the most famous volunteers

174

of the war; his writings reflect an intense, almost incredible belief in the romance of the cause. He found the death that he wished by dying during a Foreign Legion charge against German positions.

Seibert, A. *Trip to Germany during Wartime.* New York: Seibert, 1915.

Sheahan, Henry [Henry Bestor]. *A Volunteer Poilu.* Boston: Houghton, Mifflin, 1916.
An American college boy who enlisted as a volunteer ambulance driver describes some of the brutal scenes in the hospitals; he is realistic, but not bitter.

Shepherd, William Gunn. *Confessions of a War Correspondent.* New York: Harper, 1917.
An United Press International reporter tells of his life on the Western Front.

Sinclair, May. *Journal of Impressions in Belgium.* New York: Macmillan, 1915.
This records the experiences of an American woman who volunteered to drive a Belgian ambulance; during her seventeen days at the Front, she seemed to be mainly interested in collecting impressions for one of her novels.

Smith, Annie Swan. *Englishwoman's Home.* New York: Doran, 1918.
This is a collection of letters to the publisher, George Doran, on how much and how bravely England has suffered in the war.

Smith, F. B. *Observations in France.* New York: Association Press, 1918.
A Y.M.C.A. "secretary's" front-line "inspirational" experiences with the A.E.F.

Smith, Joseph L. *Over There and Back in Three Uniforms: Being the Experiences of an American Boy in the Canadian, British and American Armies at the Front and through No Man's Land.* New York: Dutton, 1918.
It is somewhat redundant to elaborate on the extended title, but the narrator was an ex-cowboy who was stimulated to join the Allies because of the Hun atrocities; even the blood and mud of Flanders do not dim his enthusiasm.

Soldier of France to His Mother: Letters from the Trenches on the Western Front. Chicago: McClurg, 1917.
These letters, although they express the usual romantic sentiments, are most notable for a remarkable, romantic attachment to nature.

Sommers, Cecil. *Temporary Heroes.* New York: Lane, 1917.
A Scottish trooper describes the filth and death of the trenches, but gives a humorous orientation to his impressions.

Spencer, Carita. *War Scenes I Shall Never Forget.* New York: Spencer, 1917.
All profits from the sale of this volume went to a war relief fund. The narrator was the guest of the Belgian queen, and was given an extended view of the Front, even being allowed to participate in some hospital work. Her outlook is completely innocent, for she has no conception of military affairs and believes that the Front is "jolly."

Spiegel, von, and Peckelsheim, Edgar. *Adventures of U-202: An Actual Narrative.* New York: Century, 1917.
This is the tale of a German submarine; the Prussian hubris shown by the crew must have infuriated American readers.

Steege, Klyda Richardson. *We of Italy.* New York: Dutton, 1917.
Epistolary in form, this narrative presents the war as a Holy Crusade, complete with the anachronistic glory of banners and fixed bayonets; the narrator was an American civilian.

Sterne, Elaine, ed. *Over the Seas for Uncle Sam*. New York: Britton, 1918.
The narrator, a first lieutenant in the Girl's National Honor Guard, relates the thrilling stories that she heard while engaged in American naval relief work.

Stevenson, William Yorke. *At the Front in a Flivver*. Boston: Houghton Mifflin, 1917.
This is the record of a Philadelphia reporter who went to France to find adventure, and found it in driving an ambulance.

————. *From Poilu to Yank*. Boston: Houghton Mifflin, 1918.
The narrator presents the story of the American ambulance volunteers who were integrated into the A.E.F. There are many vivid combat scenes, including some good descriptions of Verdun.

Stidger, William L. *Soldier Silhouettes on Our Front*. New York: Scribner's, 1918.
A Y.M.C.A. worker with the A.E.F. writes on salvation, spiritual renaissance and good fun in the American forces; thoroughly naïve.

Stimson, Julia C. *Finding Themselves*. New York: Macmillan, 1918.
A nurse from Washington University, St. Louis, describes her duties with the A.E.F.

Stobart, Mabel Annie. *Flaming Sword in Serbia and Elsewhere*. New York: Doran, 1917.
This records the strenuous life of a South African Volunteer Nurse, her capture by the Germans, her escape and her final journey to the Serbian front.

Stoddard, F. R. *War Time France*. New York: Moffat, Yard, 1918.

The record of a major in the U.S. Coast Artillery who was sent to France to gather information on innovations in anti-aircraft weaponry. Antiaircraft gunnery is the "greatest sport in the world."

Sunny Subaltern. New York: Doran, 1916.

Sutherland, Millicent. *Six Weeks at the War.* Chicago: McClurg, 1915.
This narrative presents a record of the Dutchess of Sutherland's *nobless oblige* via her work with a volunteer ambulance corps in Belgium.

Sven, Hedin. *With the German Armies in the West,* trans. H. C. de Walterstorff. New York: Lane, 1915.
Written by a German-educated Swede, this is one of the few pro-German narratives published in America. It was not well received in America, the *Dial*, for example, criticizing its glossing over German atrocities in Belgium.

Swan, Carroll Judson. *My Company.* Boston: Houghton Mifflin, 1918.
The author, an engineer captain with the A.E.F., expressed his optimism over the war itself and the quality of American soldiers.

Swayne, Martin Lutrell. *In Mesapotamia.* New York: Doran, 1918.
The narrative consists of vivid hospital sketches by a Royal Medical Corps officer in Mesopotamia.

Sweetser, Arthur. *Roadside Glimpses of the Great War.* New York: Macmillan, 1916.
A Boston newspaperman records how he was captured by the Germans and eventually released; totally anti-German and strongly for American "Preparedness."

Taylor, N. R., ed. *Heart Messages from the Trenches.* New York: Shores, 1917.

"Temporary Gentleman" in France. New York: Putnam, 1918.
Epistolary in form, this narrative contains realistic, enthusiastic descriptions of trench life by an anonymous British officer in France.

Therese, Josephine. *With Old Glory in Berlin: The Story of an American Girl's Life and Trials in Germany and her Escape from the Huns.* Boston: Page, 1918.
The author carefully tells her readers that Germans in general are fine, but that the Prussians are intrinsically evil and are ruling Germany.

Thurstan, V. *Field Hospital and Flying Column.* New York: Putnam, 1915.
The horror of war only slightly dims an English nun's enthusiasm for the glamour and excitement of action.

Tiplady, Thomas. *Cross at the Front.* New York: Revell, 1917.
A British chaplain gives his exceedingly romantic impressions of the spiritual uplift being experienced by the British soldiers who are fighting for Christ.

————. *The Soul of the Soldier: Sketches from the Western BattleFront.* New York: Revell, 1918.
An elaboration of the above. This is the type of narrative that nauseated men such as John Dos Passos, Robert Graves and Siegfried Sassoon.

Toland, E. D. *Aftermath of Battle.* New York: Macmillan, 1916.
A Princeton man who was with the Red Cross in France from 1914–1915 writes a very gentlemanly account of his activities; introduction by Owen Wister.

Told in the Huts. New York: Stokes, 1917.
The proceeds of this book were to go to the Y.M.C.A., so the religious/patriotic content of the sketches is to be expected.

Trounce, Harry Davis. *Fighting the Boche Underground.* New York: Scribner's, 1918.
An American in the British "Sappers," and later a captain of engineers in the A.E.F., gives some fearful descriptions of underground mining operations, but his writing shows an overall enthusiasm for the job.

Truitt, C. *Wartime Letters from Italy.* New York: Sherwood Press, 1915.

Turczynowicz, Laura de Gozdawa. *When the Prussians Came to Poland: The Experiences of an American Woman during the German Invasion.* New York: Putnam, 1916.
When the Germans invaded, they destroyed the sylvan bliss of an American art student who married a Polish nobleman and then settled down to manage his lush estate. There are some modifications to the usual Prussian horror stories, such as when a German doctor refused to operate on her dying child until he was first paid.

Valentini, E. *Letters and Drawings.* Boston: Houghton Mifflin, 1918.

Van Dyke, Henry. *Fighting for Peace.* New York: Scribner's, 1917.
The author held the Chair of English Literature at Princeton, but resigned to become the American minister to Holland. The narrative is a record of his diplomatic duties, and since it was published after the American entry into the war, it is much concerned with the German "plot." One would expect more from a narrator with such credentials than a narrative which casts Kaiser Wilhelm as the chief "Werewolf" in a dreadful morality play.

Van Vorst, Marie. *War Letters of an American Woman.* New York: Lane, 1916.
A description of French suffering and gallantry by an American woman abroad.

Vickers, Leslie. *Training for the Trenches.* New York: Doran, 1917.
Designed to help the new Doughboy, this volume contains a detailed description of how the author survived in the British trenches on the Western Front for two years.

Waddington, Mary Alsop. *My War Diary.* New York: Scribner's, 1917.
A French widow of a high-ranking diplomat tells of French courage and of German barbarism.

"Wagger," (pseud.). *Battery Flashes.* New York: Dutton, 1916.
This is an extremely detailed description of army life by a Royal Field artillery recruit. Obviously an educated man, he manages to read *Punch* while under fire; his loudest complaint is, " 'Rum world, isn't it.' "

Wakefield, H. R. *Fortnight at the Front.* New York: Longmans, 1915.

Waldo, Fullerton L. *America at the Front.* New York: Dutton, 1918.
The author was a reporter for the Philadelphia *Public Ledger* (*Inquirer*), which published much of the narrative in its pages. He observed some eary action at Château-Thierry, and has much praise for the Adamic spirit of Americans.

Walker, Henry Francis Bell. *Doctor's Diary in Damaraland.* New York: Longmans, 1917.
This is an unusual narrative in that it describes the war in Germany's African colonies; there is more on the medical aspect than on the military picture.

Ward, Herbert. *Mr. Poilu.* New York: Doran, 1917.
After lecturing in America for the French cause, this American author wrote this description of his ambulance work with the French.

Ward, Mrs. Humphry. *England's Effort: Letters to an American Friend.* New York: Scribner's, 1917.
The author, a famous British novelist, presents a vast apology for England in the war, including a lengthy description of the courage of English women. Designed to influence American thinking toward the war, it was popular and went through six editions in America.

———. *Towards the Goal.* New York: Scribner's, 1917.
A continuation of the first volume, it was written after America entered the war, and carries a preface by Teddy Roosevelt. She avows, "To try and make more people . . . in America realize . . . what it is we are really fighting for."

Warren, Maude Lavinia. *White Flame of France.* Boston: Small, Maynard, 1918.
After touring France, this established writer of American fiction created this narrative which treats with flowery pathos the ruin of France. Her other work includes such novels as *Barbara's Marriage* (1915).

Washburn, Stanley. *The Russian Advance.* New York: Doubleday, 1917.
The author, a correspondent for the London *Times*, gives an essentially journalistic account of the "splendid morale" of the Russian soldiers.

———. *The Russian Campaign, April to August, 1915.* New York: Scribner's, 1915.
In the first volume of the series, the author is a "Special Correspondent for the New York *Times*." The author is ostensibly neutral, but it is easy to see his strong Allied sympathies. There are many excellent photographs of the Russian front.

————. *Victory in Defeat: The Agony of Warsaw and the Russian Retreat*. New York: Doubleday, 1916.
This volume is decidedly less optimistic about Russia's chances than is the first volume. As in his other narratives, however, the narrator is strongly pro-Russian and in favor of American "Preparedness."

Watson, William Henry Lowe. *Adventures of a Despatch Rider*. New York: Dodd, Mead, 1916.
A record in epistolary form of a young British soldier who volunteered for hazardous motorcycle duty.

Watt, Lanchlan Maclean. *Heart of a Soldier*. New York: Doran, 1918.
A British army chaplain describes, sentimentally, the Christian spirit of the Allied soldiers.

Wellman, Walter Augustus. *Go, Get 'Em*. Boston: Page, 1918.
"The true adventure of an American aviator of the Lafayette flying corps who was the only Yankee flyer fighting over General Pershing's boys of the Rainbow Division in Lorraine, when they first went 'over the top.'"

Wells, Clifford Almon. *From Montreal to Vimy Ridge*. New York: Doran, 1917.
This narrative consists of a Canadian lad's letters home to his mother; although they frequently mention the cause, the letters are rather personal and not notably romantic.

Wharton, Edith. *Fighting France*. New York: Scribner's, 1915.
The famous American writer describes an extremely graceful visit to Paris and, complete with picnic basket, to the Front. Occasionally she loses control and her anti-German sentiment overflows.

What I Found Out in the House of a German Prince: By an English-American Governess. New York: Burt, 1915.
Her "revelations" on German *Kultur* and militarism reinforce the common stereotype; anonymous authorship.

Wheeler, Curtis. *Letters from an American Soldier to his Father.* Indianapolis: Bobbs-Merrill, 1918.
A second lieutenant writes to his father, the editor of *Current Opinion*, about the adventure of A.E.F. life.

Whitaker, Herman. *Hunting the German Shark: The American Navy in the Underseas War.* New York: Century, 1918.
A civilian observer with the United States destroyer force, the narrator glorifies the thrill of searching for enemy submarines.

Whitehair, Charles W. *Out There.* New York: Appleton, 1918.
An American Y.M.C.A. official in France writes of the Godly sacrifice of the American soldiers, and on how war leads to spiritual growth; there is a section on vice versus the "Y."

————. *Pictures Burned into My Memory.* New York: Saalfield, 1918.
Essentially the same in orientation as the first volume, this narrative also eulogizes the American soldier in France.

Whitehouse, J. H. *Belgium in War.* New York: Putnam, 1915.

Wile, Frederic William. *Assault.* Indianapolis: Bobbs-Merrill, 1916.
An Anglo-American press correspondent in Berlin, the narrator was arrested and then returned to America; he places the blame for the war on Germany, but he is not as vehement in his blame as are most narrators.

Williams, Albert Rhys. *In the Claws of the German Eagle.* New York: Dutton, 1917.
A Boston minister, caught in Belgium when the war started, states quite honestly that he witnessed no atrocities, but he does register contempt for the Germans.

Williams, J. E. Hoddard. *One Young Man.* New York: Doran, 1917.
This is the record of an English clerk who, though wounded at the Somme and invalided home, found his spiritual reality in war.

Williams, M. *July and August of 1914.* Cleveland: Brooks, 1915.
Privately printed.

Williams, Wythe. *Passed by the Censor.* New York: Dutton, 1916.
This is the record of the Paris correspondent of the New York *Times* during the early days of the war.

Wilmot, Mrs. Frank, ed. *Oregon Boys in the War.* Portland, Oregon: Glass and Prudhomme, 1918.
The editor collects some good war quotes by famous figures, some interesting and naïve letters from the boys in the A.E.F., and some extraordinarily bad poetry.

Wilson, L. B. *America—Here and Over There.* New York: Abingdon Press, 1918.
Marketed by the Methodist Book Concern, this is a positive attestation to the spiritual elevation of American troops.

Winnifrith, Douglas P. *Church in the Fighting Line with General Smith-Dorrien at the Front.* New York: Doran, 1916.
A Church of England front-line chaplain describes the courage and spiritual devotion of the Tommy.

Winslow, Carroll Dana. *With the French Flying Corps*. New York: Scribner's, 1916.
An United States enlistee in the Foreign Legion gleefully describes the excitement and chivalry of combat flying.

Wister, Owen. *The Pentecost of Calamity*. New York: Macmillan, 1915.
Having toured Germany, the noted author of the American West describes how the Prussian system has destroyed most of what was good in Germany. As the title suggests, he predicts that the forces of the Kaiser will suffer just retribution.

With my Regiment from the Aisne to la Bassee. Philadelphia: Lippincott, 1916.
A anonymous narrative by an English lieutenant, this is a rather light account of the action that he saw on the Western Front.

With the R.A.M.C. in Egypt. New York: Funk and Wagnalls, 1918.

Wonderful Stories: Winning the V.C. in the Great War. New York: Dutton, 1918.
The anonymous editor collects melodramatic and flamboyant exploits by Allied soldiers.

Wood, Eric Fisher. *The Note-Book of an Attaché*. New York: Century, 1915.
The author was a courier for the American embassy in Paris. Later, he became a volunteer with the American Ambulance Corps; strongly in favor of American "Preparedness."

————. *The Note-Book of an Intelligence Officer*. New York: Century, 1917.
After touring Germany and Austria, the narrator lost any vestige of neutrality and became a Major in the British army.

He carried letters of introduction from Teddy Roosevelt and Leonard Wood.

Wood, Walter. *In the Line of Battle*. New York: Brentano's, 1916.

————. *Soldier's Stories of the War*. New York: Brentano's, 1915.
This is an anthology containing many heroism stories from the Western Front; unselective in nature, it contains many cheaply exciting tales.

Wounded and a Prisoner of War, by an Exchange Officer. New York: Doran, 1917.
The anonymous narrator was a regular army captain with the British forces, and the narrative is extremely professional in tone. He does not emphasize German mistreatment of prisoners.

Wright, Jack Morris. *A Poet of the Air*. Boston: Houghton Mifflin, 1918.
A Harvard man who was killed in the A.E.F. aviation section, the narrator writes of acts of intense excitement and conscious sacrifice. He was only nineteen when he was shot down.

Yerta, Gabrielle, Mand Marguerita. *Six Women and the Invasion*. Boston: Houghton Mifflin, 1918.
Although they relate few Hun horror stories, the women narrators do tell of the undesirability of living behind the German lines in France.

Young, Geoffrey Winthrop. *From the Trenches: Louvain to the Aisne*. New York: Stokes, 1915.
An English correspondent describes the wreck of Belgium by the Germans, and emphasizes the splendid fighting qualities of the British army.

SECONDARY SOURCES

Books

Bond, Georges. *Verdun,* trans. Frances Frenage. New York: Macmillan, 1960.

Brophy, John, ed. *The Long Trail: What the Soldiers Said and Sang in 1914–1918.* London: London House, 1965.

Chase, Richard. *The American Novel and Its Traditions.* New York: Doubleday, 1957.

Congdon, Donald, ed. *Combat: World War I.* New York: Dial, 1965.

Crozier, Emmet. *American Reporters on the Western Front, 1914–1918.* New York: Oxford University Press, 1959.

Dos Passos, John. *Mr. Wilson's War.* New York: Doubleday, 1962.

Fitzgerald, F. Scott. *Tender is the Night.* New York: Scribner's, 1933.

Fogle, Richard Harter. *The Romantic Movement in American Writing.* New York: Odyssey, 1966.

Ford, Ford Madox. *Between Saint Dennis and Saint George.* New York: Hodder and Stoughton, 1915.

Freidel, Frank. *Over There: The Story of America's First Great Crusade.* Boston: Little, Brown, 1964.

Graves, Robert. *Good-bye to All That.* New York: Cape and Smith, 1929.

Levin, David. *History as Romantic Art.* Stanford: Stanford University Press, 1959.

Lewis, R. W. B. *The American Adam.* Chicago: University of Chicago Press, 1955.

Mason, Herbert Molly, Jr. *The Lafayette Escadrille.* New York: Random House, 1964.

Matthews, William, and Dixon Wecter. *Our Soldiers Speak, 1775–1918.* Boston: Little, Brown, 1943.

May, Ernest. *The World War and American Isolation, 1914–1917.* Cambridge, Mass.: Harvard University Press, 1959.

May, Henry F. *The End of American Innocence, 1912–1917.* New York: Knopf, 1959.

Millis, Walter. *Road to War: America, 1914–1917.* Boston: Houghton Mifflin, 1935.

Nichols, Robert, ed. *Anthology of War Poetry.* London: Nicholson and Watson, 1943.

Parsons, I. M., ed. *Men Who March Away.* New York: Viking, 1965.

Pitt, Barrie. *1918: The Last Act.* New York: Norton, 1964.

Sassoon, Siegfried. *The Memoirs of an Infantry Officer.* New York: Doubleday, 1938.

Smith, Daniel M. *The Great Departure: The United States and World War I, 1914–1920.* New York: Wiley, 1965.

Stallings, Laurence. *The Doughboys.* New York: Harper and Row, 1963.

Tuchman, Barbara. *The Guns of August.* New York: Dell, 1962.

————. *The Zimmerman Telegram.* New York: Delta, 1963.

Watt, Richard. *Dare Call It Treason.* New York: Simon and Schuster, 1963.

Wilson, Woodrow. *In Our First Year of War: Messages and Addresses to the Congress and the People, March 5, 1917, to January 8, 1918.* New York: Harper, 1918.

Wolff, Leon. *In Flanders Field.* New York: Ballantine, 1958.

Periodicals

Evans, B. I. "Goodbye to What?" *Spectator*, CXLIV (February, 1922), 267–268.

Kelly, R. "Ten Real War Books," *Dial*, LXII (March 8, 1917), 96–98.

New York Times, 1918.

Northup, C. S. "War and Literature," *Sewanee Review*, XXV (July, 1917), 339–347.

"Notable Recent War Books." (anon. rev.), *Literary Digest*, LXVI (April 13, 1918), 38–43.

Ogg, Frederic A. "America and the Great War," *Dial*, LVIII (April 29, 1915), 337–340.

———. "New Books about the War," *Dial*, LVIII (January 16, 1915), 44–47.

"Popular War Books," (anon. rev.), *Literary Digest*, LII (January 22, 1916), 176.

Rice, Wallace. "Scorched with the Flames of War," *Dial*, LVIX (June 24, 1915), 22–26.

"A Shelf of War Books." (anon. rev.), *Independent*, LXXXIV (November 1, 1915), 194–195.

Smith, R. L. "Some Bibliographies of the European War and Its Causes," *Bulletin of Bibliography*, Vol. X, no. 3 (July, 1918), 50–52.

Stearns, Harold. "Pro-Allies," *New Republic*, IX (November 18, 1916), 24–30.

Thurston, Carl H. P. "Is the Pen Swifter than the Sword?" *Bookman*, XLVI (November, 1917), 286–291.

Tillinghurst, Philip. "From the War-Time Bookshelf," *Bookman*, XLI (May, 1915), 329–334.

"War Books and War." (anon. rev.), *Spectator*, CXLIV (May, 1930), 773–774.

Unpublished Material

Clough, Wilson Ober. Unpublished letters to the author, January 15, 1965, and March 19, 1965.

———. Unpublished letter to the author, April 26, 1967.

Conner, James R. "Pen and Sword: World War I Novels in America, 1916–1941." Unpublished Ph.D. dissertation, University of Wisconsin, 1961.

Critoph, Gerald E. "The American Literary Reaction to World War I." Unpublished Ph.D. dissertation, University of Pennsylvania, 1957.

INDEX

McClure's Magazine, 2

Manliness, 40–42, 64–66, 80, 82–84

March, Peyton C., 56

March, William, 21

Marine Corps, U.S., 74

Marne, Battle of, 18

Mauldin, Bill, 19

May, Henry F., 3

Millis, Walter, 38

Morale, of Troops, 19

Morality, War and, 28

Motley, John L., 5

Muckrakers, 2

Mutinies, in French Army, 5, 34

Myth, American Agrarian, 17

Narratives; Popularity of, 102–105; and Intelligensia, 102

Nature, Admiration of, 75, 107; Destruction of, 39

Neutrality, American, 26, 27

New Freedom, 2

Nichols, Robert, 103

Northrup, Clark S., 104

Norton-Harjes Corps, 51, 65

Objectors, Conscientious, 32

Optimism, Allied, 58

Page, Walter, 38

Parkman, Francis, 5, 105

Parsons, I. M., 53

Patriotism, American, 27, 57–58, 60–61, 107

Pell, E. L., 58

Perry, Thomas Sergeant, 103

Pershing, General John, 86–87

Pierce, Waldo, 51

Porter, Eleanor H., 3

Powell, E. A., 86

Preparedness, in America, 12, 33

Prescott, William H., 5

Propaganda, in America, 14, 78, 100

Prussia, Nature of People, 16, 20, 29, 77, 91

Punch Magazine, 14

Pyle, Ernie, 19

Red Cross, Volunteers in, 28

Regiments, English and Canadian: Argyll and Sutherland Highlanders, 35; Black Watch, 81; Guards, 50; London Scottish, 73; Yorkshire Light Infantry, 18

Religion, of Soldiers, 11, 12, 18, 31, 32, 33, 45–46, 64–67, 71–72, 85

Remarque, Erich Maria, 21

Renaissance, Moral and Spiritual, 13, 19, 32, 34, 43–46, 64, 69–70, 72, 85, 107

Repplier, Agnes, 29

Rheims, Cathedral of, 20

Richthofen, Manfred Freiberr von, 78, 90

Robinson, Edwin Arlington, 103

Romanticism, in Narratives, 4, 6, 7, 9, 10, 11, 13, 14, 15, 17, 18, 20, 30, 39, 42, 47–48, 50, 53, 61, 73, 92, 93, 94–95, 104–108

Roosevelt, Theodore, 10, 27, 29, 58, 69, 84, 97

CHARLES V. GENTHE

Charles V. Genthe's interest in the narratives of World War I grew from his research in American studies at Washington State University, where he received his doctorate. He was graduated *magna cum laude* from Rutgers University in 1959 and has taught at Miami-Dade Junior College in Florida and at Long Beach State College, as well as Chico State College in Chico, California where he now lives and works as an associate professor of English and coordinator of American studies.

Professor Genthe has contributed articles to a number of journals and is at work on an anthology of American literature to be published in 1970 by Blaisdell. He is married and a captain in the United States Army Reserve.